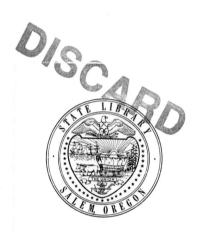

SOUNDS FOR SILENTS

by
Charles Hofmann

Foreword   Lillian Gish

DBS Publications/Drama Book Specialists
New York, New York

Published in the United States of America
DBS Publications, Inc./Drama Book Specialists
Library of Congress Catalog Card Number: 74-107465
SBN: 910482-14-4

For JESSIE
who has seen lots of movies
with my sounds for silents

This book is for those interested in creating music for early films, for those who are interested in hearing the music for these films, and for those who wish to know something about musical backgrounds during the decades when sounds were created for silents.

Grateful thanks to Lillian Gish for her interest and enthusiasm in my work, and for her heartfelt foreword.

The recording was made by my editor, Ralph Pine, at the Museum of Modern Art, with the assistance of Mary Yushak, Jed Horne, and Jessie Macartney-Filgate.

William Penn deserves special acknowledgment for his contribution of the musical transcriptions of my original film scores. The transcriptions were made from tapes recorded at the Museum, many of them during screenings with audiences. Dr. Penn's original piano score for *Rescued from an Eagle's Nest* is included herein in its entirety, an example of music by a young modern composer creating new background for early films.

The following friends and correspondents who also contributed to this volume must be mentioned:

Herman G. Weinberg	William K. Everson
William Sloan	David Mendoza
Lois Wilson	Blanche Sweet
Anita Loos	Neil Hamilton
Marian Murray	James Beveridge
Mary Yushak	Ernest D. Burns
Edward Wagenknecht	Bert Ennis
Max Schaffner	Fritz Lang
George C. Pratt	Arthur Steiger
Colleen Moore	Betty Bronson
Paul Killiam	Andrew McKay

The staff of the Department of Film at the Museum of Modern Art; the staff of the Library at the Museum;

G. Schirmer, *Harper's Bazaar*, Elkan-Vogel Company, for quotations and musical reproductions from their publications;

Films in Review for permission to quote from Theodore Huff's article, "Chaplin as Composer";

Decca Records for allowing the reproduction of the album cover for *The Chaplin Revue;*

Jay Leyda for sending pages from Meisel's original scores for *Potemkin* and *October,* recently discovered in Berlin;

Staff of the Drama Book Shop in New York;

and to the many who attended screenings at the Museum of Modern Art and talked to me about the music.

CHARLES HOFMANN
New York City
1969

"... It all started with the pianist in the early movie theatres. He has become a part of history, often quoted, imitated, laughed at, and parodied. To most people of my age, the sound of the piano in the nickelodeons is a cherished childhood memory. . . .

The fact remains that the silent movie needed music as a dry cereal needs cream."

KURT WEILL
in *Harper's Bazaar,* 1946

"... The movies do need music, and need it badly. By itself the screen is a pretty cold proposition. . . . Music is like a small flame put under the screen to help warm it. . . . Film music makes sense only if it helps the films; no matter how good, distinguished, or successful, the music must be secondary in importance to the story being told on the screen."

AARON COPLAND
in *Modern Music,* 1940

FOREWORD

To tell a story in pictures, accompanied solely by music, is difficult. It is a form more challenging than that with spoken words, which at best is bastard theatre. The silent film with music is almost entirely a 20th century product. Nothing like it had ever been seen before. Here was truly a new art form. The age-old art of the theatre, based on the author's words to reveal his plots and thoughts, spoken from a stage by players who are lighted and framed by the scenery of designers, is a vastly different art. In the silent film, earth and sky could dwarf most scenery, and music was used to frame and enhance the story being told.

When we made the silent film version of *La Bohème*, the estate of Puccini was in litigation, making it impossible for us to use his music. A substitute score composed by Messrs. David Mendoza and William Axt was beautiful. The famous critic, George Jean Nathan, said he thought it better than the one being sung at the Metropolitan Opera. It contributed greatly to the long runs enjoyed by that sad story.

No one today seems to understand this better than Charles Hofmann.

Today, his music for this same film has the same effect.

When I see old films run at the Museum of Modern Art here in New York, he uses his enormous musical repertory to heighten the mood of each scene. He memorizes the film and the music, blending the changes so adroitly that you, watching, are unaware of how the intense vibrations of these sounds are created. Only when it is over, do you realize how your mind has been caught and held captive by what you have seen and heard.

The art of theatre is seen and heard from too great a distance to look into the eyes of players and read their thoughts. On stage the voice, almost unaided, must reveal emotion, whereas the camera can be so intimate that it can give something like an x-ray of the human psyche. John Barrymore, who knew both arts well, said that if the camera held your face on screen long enough, it would not only reveal what you had for breakfast, but tell who your ancestors were.

Many of our modern films seem to be returning to the purer form of telling a story in motion pictures, depending upon music and animation rather than words. No doubt there are minds at work now with enough creative imagination to convert film into a universal language understood by everyone everywhere. What an enormous force and help it would be if each one involved took the responsibility for what he was saying. Such power goes far beyond the printed word. It could show the problems, work out solutions, or at least clarify, simplify and lead to helpful, even peaceful, understanding. Then those films with music could be sent around the world as the Universal Esperanto!

LILLIAN GISH
New York
1969

NO FILMS WERE SILENT

Since the earliest days of the movies there has really been no such thing as a "silent film." Music was always an integral part of the showing of motion pictures, inseparable from the visual, indispensable as accompaniment to films.

When the Lumière brothers exhibited their first films in Paris in 1895, these films were accompanied by piano improvisations based on popular tunes. During this period Georges Méliès, Thomas Edison, and other early film makers used music with their exhibitions.

Thomas Edison became interested in developing his new invention that would project "living pictures" after he came to believe it would do for the eye what the phonograph did for the ear. Edison never dissociated his phonograph from his films. In 1887 he began to work with W. K. L. Dickson on experiments "aimed at putting eyes into the phonograph."* When his pictures were shown, Edison's cylinders played music simultaneously, because many of them were recorded at the time the films were made. More than a quarter of a century later this idea was developed into modern sound film by the Vitaphone and later

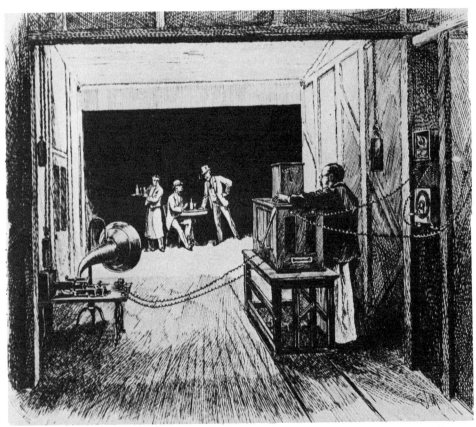

The interior of the Kinetographic Theater, Edison's laboratory, Orange, New Jersey, showing phonograph and kinetograph. The recording apparatus from artist's drawing, is a clear illustration of the attempts to create sound film. The Edison laboratory experimented with several musical subjects and some of these films are still in existence.

(from **Century Magazine,** June 1894)

processes. Edison believed so strongly in this idea that he wrote: "I believe that in coming years . . . grand opera can be given at the Metropolitan Opera House . . . without any material change from the original, and with artists and musicians long since dead."

To be sure, the first commercially exhibited moving pictures were shown in vaudeville houses, music halls, cafés, or at fairgrounds and in lecture halls, and so musicians were usually available to play for the rest of the program. Music has always been tied in with dramatic and other entertainment, and has been associated with the theatre since ancient days. It was natural that it be associated with films from the beginning.

In those earliest days, the music bore little relationship to what people saw on the screen. Any type of music seemed appropriate and sufficient. Kurt London writes of the accompanist: "His repertory remained a matter of complete indifference; he played anything he liked, and there was little or no connection between the music and the film it accompanied."**

Since the story of these beginnings has been told many times, sources for this history are listed in the bibliography. To see primitive beginnings today, one is referred to such "documentary" excerpts as those found in *Origins of the Motion Picture,*** produced by the U. S. Navy in 1955, based on the book *Magic Shadows* by Martin Quigley, Jr.

At the turn of the century, when house musicians made music to accompany films, there were also sound-effects men stationed back of the screen to add realism to the scenes. Train bells and whistles, fire engine bells, gun shots, the whirring of wind machines, explosions, cannon fire, and many other sounds would be heard, it was hoped, at the same moment they were seen on the screen. Sometimes such realism was so effective that the early movie audiences were frightened and would empty the house in a few seconds flat. Startling scenes of realism had a dynamic effect, and people could not believe that what they saw was not really happening.

However, in the earliest days of the film, the musicians sat in front of the screen just as they did when playing for the vaudeville acts in the same houses. That arrangement continued when theatres were especially built for the movies, and musicians played in the pit—piano, organ or orchestra—until the coming of the sound film.

At first, one must remember, there was little relationship between the music and the picture. The house musician usually played what he liked, or what he already knew. Lively music to a solemn scene was a common experience during those first years. More often the same music was heard for every picture and there was little differentiation between one film and another. It was as if the musicians never watched the screen!

When film-making and film-going became more serious, such incongruity became apparent and the musicians became more serious also, taking some care with the mood, and trying to match their selections of music to the scenes and continuity of action.

Set pieces became standard, and the musician tried to extend his repertory so that the accompaniment would not become monotonous. A catalog of such a repertory gradually became a working library for the movie musician, and the possibilities of utilizing the material may be found in this book on the pages devoted to musical moods and cue sheets.

And in those earliest days (especially around and after 1910) the movie house musician was a very important man. He often played the same musical motifs for similar types of episodes that flashed across the screen. There were pleasant strains, sad, lively, dramatic and bright strains, and the pianist played on and on until the film ended. This sort of thing, oftentimes with extra added instruments or later even a large orchestra, was seen and heard in hundreds of movie houses across the country for many years, until the coming of sound films, the "talkie," and what was then called "canned music." After that, the silent movie musicians seemed to disappear.

Occasionally one of those versatile musicians would be heard at film festivals, or in schools, libraries, or museums, when early films were screened. It is this versatile musician who concerns us in this book, because we are interested in music for early films when screened today for modern audiences. Creative musicians are neeeded to keep these important traditions alive and make early films more meaningful to today's audiences.

° *Preface to* History of the Kinetograph, Kinetoscope and Kinetophonograph *by Dickson & Dickson, 1895. The story of this venture is told in Gordon Hendrick's* The Edison Motion Picture Myth *(1961) and in Terry Ramsaye's* A Million and One Nights *(1926).*

°° *London,* Film Music *(London, Faber & Faber, 1936), p. 40.*

°°° *Film circulated by the Museum of Modern Art Film Library.*

BANNER PRODUCTIONS, Inc. Present
"The Checkered Flag"
with ELAINE HAMMERSTEIN
TAX FREE AND TAXABLE
DESCRIPTIVE FILMUSIC GUIDE
By MICHAEL HOFFMAN

Timing based on a speed of 11 minutes per 1000 feet (55 minutes)

Cue	Appearing on Film	Time Min.	Descriptive Action of Each Scene	Tempo of Action & Music Required	COMPOSITION SUGGESTIONS (1st) *Tax Free (2nd) **Taxable.
T	At screening of titles	3	Neutral	2/4 Moderato	
T	Jack Reese—who left	3	Romantic	4/4 Romance THEME	*Song of Ramance (Hoffman) THEME **Tea Rose (MacDowell) THEME
T	The Corbin Plant	5	Neutral	4/4 Moderato	*Love's Fantasy (Frommel) **Thoughts of Yore (Frey)
S	Girl motions thru window	4½	Brisk	6/8 Allegretto	*Sweet Lavender (Wheeler) **Debutante (Axt)
T	J. Gordon Andrews	5	Dramatic	4/4 Dramatic	*Turbulent Tensions (Hoffman) **Recitative No. 1 (Levy)
T	Mother McGuire's Boarding	4½	Comical	2/4 Allegretto	*Frolics and Youth (Maykels) **Spirit of Youth (Dahlquist)
T	Barton's Home—where	2	Neutral	2/4 Moderato	*Forget-Me-Not (Macbeth) **Pub. Ascher **Pub. Fischer
S	Eyes spy thru hole	3	Exciting P—F Action	2/4 Agitato P—F Action	*Disturbance (Hoffman) **Rustic Allegro (Savino)
T	Rita braves her father's	5	Romantic	THEME	*THEME **THEME
T	That night—	3	Jazz dance	2/4 Fox Trot	*My Sugar (Snyder) **Yearning (Davis)
S	Reese and girl into room Drum play 2/4 on dance scenes	4	Mystery and Jazz	2/4 Agitato	*Pangs of Passion (Wagner) **Rage (Axt)
S	Hooded man sneaks around	3	Mysterious	4/4 Mysterioso	*Loitering Shadows (Hoffman) **Weird Myst. (Kilenyi)
T	What a man	2½	Excitement	2/4 Agitato	*Distress (Breil) **Thrills (Sanders)
S	Frenchman opens auto door Drum play 2/4 on dance scenes	4	Mystery and Jazz	2/4 Agitato	*Destruction (Hoffman) **Hurry 33 (Minot)
T	There's where I	4	Mysterious	4/4 Mysterioso	*Green Vipers (Maykels) **Hurry 26 (Minot)
T	The trembling hour	5	Conspiracy	2/4 Trem. Agitato	*Trembling Anxiety (Hoffman) **Fuga (Marie)
T	I hope Jack Reese wins	4	Race starts	2/4 Galop	*Galop at Fair (Burrel) **Allegro No. 10 (Lake)
S	Frenchman in ambulance	3	Race and tumult	2/4 Furioso	*Avenging Storm (Hoffman) **Blizzard (Aborn)
S	Girl winner takes off cap	1	Romantic	THEME	*THEME **THEME

End warning (for chord finish) OLD AND YOUNG MAN SHAKE HANDS.

TAX-FREE MEANS that Theatre Owners are relieved of paying music tax.
ANY OR ALL COMPOSITIONS HEREON MENTIONED MAY BE PROCURED FROM
TAX-FREE MUSIC CO., 1674 BROADWAY, NEW YORK
AT WHOLESALE PRICES

Cue sheets were sent out with many films, with theme indications carefully timed for each scene.

MUSIC TO FIT THE PICTURES

There have been countless books and articles written about the movies in all their aspects, past and present, but very few of these books include any mention of film music. A few lines or paragraphs, possibly two or three pages at the most, seemed sufficient to cover the subject. Many of these books include a line or two—the statement that began this book—which claimed that "there has been no such thing as a silent film," or "silent films were never silent."

Lewis Jacobs devotes only one paragraph to film music in *The Rise of the American Film*, and later mentions music in connection with the coming of sound and the Vitaphone—

". . . With the enlarging of theatres and the change in the character of audiences* the music accompanying a motion picture was given careful attention. Owing principally to the successful scoring of *The Birth of a Nation*, the musical scorer became an esteemed figure in the motion picture industry almost overnight. His job was to plan the accompaniment of a picture, which was then printed in book form. . . . By 1916 only the very cheapest of movie houses did not have an orchestra instead of a pianist. . . ."**

* Circa 1912-1914 and thereafter.
** Jacobs, The Rise of the American Film (N.Y., Harcourt, Brace & Co., 1939; reprinted N.Y., Teachers College, Columbia University, 1968), p. 224.

Most of these books mentioned music only in connection with *The Birth of a Nation*. However, an important book such as Ernest Lindgren's *The Art of the Film* devoted an entire chapter to film music, but only four pages to the silent film accompaniment. The same can be said of Siegfried Kracauer's *Theory of Film*, which includes one chapter. Kevin Brownlow's *The Parade's Gone By . . .* discusses the subject (including fascinating anecdotes) in three pages, even though he devotes twenty-three pages in the same book to the filming of the 1926 *Ben-Hur*.

As several commentators have observed—"People go to see the picture, not to hear the music," though they seldom deny the importance of music as a complement to any film through the years.

Edward Wagenknecht in his charmingly nostalgic, heartfelt book, *The Movies in the Age of Innocence*, takes this view: "Although I agree with the film aestheticians who find the film more closely allied aesthetically with music than with any other art—except for a picture like *The Birth of a Nation*, which had a fine and memorable musical score which I still remember—I do not even miss the music when silent films are projected privately."*

Prof. Wagenknecht elaborated his views when I asked him, and added, "I am sure the musical score contributed to my enjoyment of many films, but I cannot now remember *what* was used, and I fear I never listened to the music *as such*. . . . Even now, when I run *The Birth* for home projection (the only score which impressed me which I remember) I cannot look at some scenes without hearing the music that went with them."**

It is interesting to note the attitudes and impressions of persons who paid special attention to this phase of development, and the following quotations are probably typical.

Paul Evert Denton writes in *Moving Picture World*, April 23, 1916, p. 638—

"Moving pictures and music are inseparable. This the public cannot deny. And yet how little attention and praise the musician at the piano receives. The musician or piano player in a moving picture show must be versatile. He should have accurate knowledge of the tunes of a catalogue of songs that have caught the public fancy. Coupled with this knowledge he must have the *power of application*. . . . The pianist must be able to quickly change his music to put the interested spectator in the mood the picture demands. He must acquire the ability of being able to play to the correct time in which the figures in the picture dance, if there is a Terpsichorean film. This is no easy matter, as the figures sometimes change the time quite frequently in a picture. The pianist must watch close, because the effect would be rather marred if a two-step were played while a Colonial minuet was being executed. . . . *Music, while it may escape the attention of the spectator, has the strange and subtle influence of creating moods, and that is why it is so important in the presentation of the moving picture.*"

Gregg A. Frelinger, a practical musician of many years of experience, compiled the book *Motion Picture Piano Music*, which had widespread use, and wrote

* *University of Oklahoma Press, 1962, p. 9.*
** *Letter to the author, December 14, 1968. He did, however, also recall a few melodies from* Way Down East *and* Orphans of the Storm.

from Lafayette, Indiana, to *Moving Picture World*—

". . . I really believe that the stand you have taken relative to 'music to fit the pictures' will have a very good and wholesome effect upon moving picture theatre managers, and that a good many will awaken to the fact that appropriate music greatly enhances the value of motion picture entertainment. . . . The articles which you have recently written . . . are a great source of enlightenment to moving picture theatre managers, and if they will follow your business 'tips' they will not have to resort to vaudeville and other expensive and useless methods. If the moving picture theatre managers would insist that their pianists try and conform their music to the picture, it would soon be noticed that the patronage of the theatre would greatly increase in numbers, superinduced by the added enjoyment and pleasure derived by having the picture properly interpreted."❋

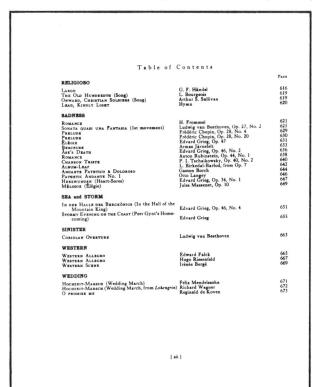

Table of Contents

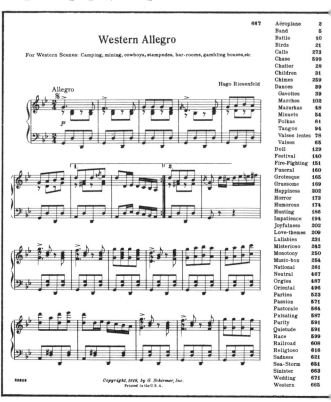

667

Western Allegro

For Western Scenes: Camping, mining, cowboys, stampedes, bar-rooms, gambling houses, *etc.*

Hugo Riesenfeld

Allegro

Copyright, 1918, by G. Schirmer, Inc.
Printed in the U. S. A.

A page from Erno Rapee's **Manual** with subject headings and typical examples selected to create the proper moods.

Another page showing the quick-reference index so essential to the performing musician who had to fit the music to almost every situation!

(Copyright 1924, G. Shirmer, Inc., used by permission)

". . . Incidental music is claiming the intelligent attention of some of the picture manufacturers, notably the Edison and the Vitagraph. Some time ago the Edison Company commenced printing programmes of instrumental music suitable for Edison releases, and recently the Vitagraph Company announced that it would

❋ *February 26, 1910. The magazine reported later that one theatre manager doubled his attendance when he hired a competent pianist.*

introduce properly arranged piano scores with each film of its manufacture. Now let some enterprising firm send along a prepared programme of sound effects to go with each subject, and another step upward will have been recorded. . . . The value of proper incidental music is well illustrated at the Keith and Proctor Union Square House, where the management pays particular attention to this feature. When the Biograph film *In Old Kentucky* was exhibited at that house the applause was more frequent throughout the reel than at the other houses where the same subject was shown, and the difference is attributed to the excellent musical selections that were used. . . . Bad judgement in the selection of music may ruin an exhibition as much as a good programme may help it. Imagine a pathetic scene showing a husband mourning his dead wife accompanied by the strains of 'No Wedding Bells for Me!' And yet this exact circumstance was noted by the writer recently. . . ."

The New York Daily Mirror,
October 9, 1909

". . . We go down again and take a seat in the auditorium to see the latest Biograph—a grand film, we are told by Mr. Hines. . . . A Pathé comedy is on, with funny chases and crushed china, the audience is shouting with delight. Here is the feature of the day, *A Fool's Revenge*, by Biograph . . . a highly dramatic subject on the theme of *Rigoletto* . . . a film that keeps one in an intense suspense from beginning to end. . . . The film made a deep impression on the audience. . . . *A pleasant variation from the eternal ragtime was a refined deliverance of classical music corresponding to the character of the picture,* including Schumann's 'Träumerei' and Beethoven's 'Moonlight Sonata.' *The first time, indeed, we ever heard Beethoven in a five-cent theater. . . .*"

Moving Picture World,
March 13, 1909

Complementary music for almost any mood was to be found in the repertory of the movie house musician. Themes for "uncanny situations," "impending disaster" or "fear" were especially composed and included in collections of **Photo-play Music.** This example might be appropriate for Jean Epstein's **The Fall of the House of Usher** (1928).

Films of American life, especially of pioneer or rural scenes, are enhanced by suggestions of folk music. Naive, simple tunes of early America are appropriate for films such as Griffith's **True Heart Susie** (1919) or King Vidor's **The Jack Knife Man** (1920).
Lillian Gish and Robert Harron in the Griffith romance.

"There is one head under which nearly every moving picture theater in New York City, in our opinion, is lamentably deficient. We mean the music—the music that accompanies, illustrates, or which is supposed to harmonize with the pictures. The piano and some sound effects are usually considered sufficient; and oh, and oh, the piano and the players we sometimes hear and sometimes see! The former is more often than not out of tune, and the latter, though he can strike the key with something like accuracy and precision, if not violence, cannot play music, or, if he can, he does not. In other words, speaking generally, the musical end of the moving picture house programme is, as a rule, so unsatisfactory that we think it our duty specially in this article to call attention to it.

"We all know the old poetical lines, 'That music hath charms to soothe the savage breast, etc.' Good music in a moving picture house can make up for a lot of deficiency in other respects. The house may be cheerless and the pictures and the manners of showing them indifferent, the song slides bad, the singing discordant, but if there is a constant stream of good music going on, either from a small orchestra or some of the automatic instruments on the market which are especially supplied for amusement places, the audience will forgive a lot. And where all else is good, the house good, the administration good, why, if there is also agreeable and suitable music, well-played music, which symphonizes, as it were, with the pictures, it bridges the intervals and generally gratifies the ear. Then the show will create an even better and more favorable impression.

"Now we ask all those responsible for the conduct of moving picture houses to pay closer attention to the musical end. Half the pianists whom we have heard these last six months deserve to lose their jobs, for if they can play, they either won't or don't. The pianos should be either burnt or put into tune or replaced with better ones. But, better still, we think, is our advice, wherever practical to engage a small orchestra of strings, with the addition of the piano and the sound effects. Of course, this costs money, but we think that the outlay would recoup itself.

". . . The object of this present article will have been gained if it is the means of drawing exhibitors to the importance of the musical end, which, at present, is not so good as it might be."

"The Musical End," editorial in
Moving Picture World,
July 3, 1909

James Cruze's **The Covered Wagon** (1923) emphasized Stephen Collins Foster's "O Suzanna!" throughout the film, first heard in the opening shot of Johnny Fox playing the banjo.
The stirring march rhythm, preceded by a bugle call, magnified the epic grandeur of the procession of wagon trains. American Indian musical themes and early American Protestant hymns also added atmosphere to this great epic film, musically scored by Hugo Riesenfeld.

Piano score from author's collection, inscribed by Lois Wilson, the "Molly Wingate" of the film, November 1968, "with great appreciation for his loyalty and interest in the old days. . . ."

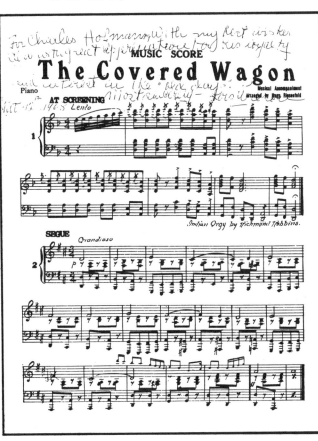

Hugo Riesenfeld, compiler and composer of many scores for important films, has this to say in his article, "Music and Motion Pictures"[*] —

"Nowadays no important picture is released without a specially prepared score. Infinite care is taken and sometimes weeks spent in the preparation of a score, so that every emotion and every bit of action on the screen will be exactly reproduced musically. As long as six months has sometimes been spent on certain of the more important scores.[**] . . . The chief difficulty in score writing is keeping the music subordinate to the action on the screen. It must never obtrude itself. The audience must never be conscious of hearing a familiar tune. . . . A good film can be made better by a good score. An inferior film does not seem nearly so bad if it has an excellent musical background. . . .

"In preparing the music for a film, the director first has the picture run off while he makes notes. He then consults his library for selections which he believes will produce the proper atmosphere. With these before him he again calls for a running off of the film, and working at a piano, he tries out the music he has selected. Now and then he presses a button which notifies the projectionist to stop the machine while he looks for a different number or makes further notes. After music is assembled and timed to the film, it is turned over to copyists who prepare a complete score for the musicians. Usually three or four days are devoted to rehearsals. . . . Very often, if the arranger cannot find satisfactory music for a certain bit of action, he is obliged to compose some himself. The musical ability required for this work is of such a high caliber that only the larger theatres are able to afford it. It cannot be expected that the musical head of a theatre in a small town will be able to write as good a score as an expert employed by a metropolitan theatre. For this reason many scores are syndicated, and sent with the film all over the world."

It seems evident that the ways and methods of accompanying film with music were much the same all over the world. Donald Ritchie, who has worked with and written about Japanese films for many years says: "During the silent film days Japanese pictures were accompanied by music, but rarely was it Japanese music. American popular tunes from both the 19th and 20th centuries were heard more often, tunes that were as popular in Japan as anywhere else. For some scenes you would often hear a Stephen Foster melody. It is only in the sound era that we find films accompanied by Japanese music with their own instruments."[***]

---

[*] *Included in* The Motion Picture and Its Economic and Social Aspects, *edited by Clyde L. King and Frank A. Tichenor,* American Academy of Political and Social Sciences Annals, *v. 128, November 1926, pp. 85–62.*

[**] *"It took five weeks for me to prepare the score for* The Big Parade *and a few weeks more than that for* Ben-Hur." *(David Mendoza in conversation with the author, New York, November 1968.)*

[***] *Donald Ritchie in conversation with the author, New York, November 1967.*

Mid-nineteenth century songs as well as Irish tunes played a great part in the atmosphere of John Ford's **The Iron Horse** (1924), with score arranged by Erno Rapee. "Drill, Ye Tarriers, Drill!" was sung by the work crew in the track laying scenes and identified three Irish characters.

Music score for Fred Niblo's **Ben-Hur** (1926) was adapted and arranged by David Mendoza and William Axt. Mendoza (in conversation with the author in New York in 1968) said, "After several screenings, the actual composition of the score took nearly six weeks." Francis X. Bushman (as Messala) is shown in the chariot race scene, with corresponding music of the race from the First Violin part.

MOODS OF MUSIC . . . THE CUE SHEET

When the Duke in *Twelfth-Night* declaimed that music perhaps was the food of love, he requested his musicians to "play on."

The moral for us in these pages is that the proper music will in turn enhance a love scene, if it is not too obvious and overdone, and is in keeping with what the moviegoer is watching on the screen. If it becomes "not so sweet," it has been overdone and the musicians have overdeveloped it or departed from the proper mood of the visual. Then when the pianist "plays on" he must be careful to follow this scene sympathetically and interpret as well as complement the action.

Fair ladies through the centuries have been stirred with music. Lovers have serenaded and accomplished their purpose with the right mood of music. Hamlet advised to "suit the action to the word" and to "let your own discretion be your tutor." Good advice for a movie musician in interpreting what he sees on the screen.

This advice applies to any mood in any film. Being alert, anticipating the continuity and the flow of action, the pianist needs to play on, dissolving from one mood to another as the film continues.

Actually one needs be an "instant composer" to anticipate and dissolve such musical moods as the film progresses. From this need evolved what we know as the "cue sheet"—planned and set pieces timed to the picture—all in keeping with the right moods.

In the beginning the musicians played what they wished, what they already knew, or what they thought best suited to the film's action. Much of it was successful, much of it was even in those early days ridiculous.* To many movie audiences it didn't seem to make much difference, but to others it seems important to have the right music at the right moment whether the music was obvious or not. In following the development of film music we must realize the importance of the "cue sheet" which actually preceded the formal, original or arranged score. Many musicians and many film companies claimed to be the "inventors" of planned music for films. These ideas must have grown simultaneously and during the second decade of the moving picture theatres the circulating of musical cue sheets and planned scores was a tremendous business.

Bert Ennis claims the inspiration for the first use of cue sheets and other musical indications in his informal article, "Music Cues—Without the Aid of Riesenfeld—in 1910."

"Everytime I catch a symphony orchestra in one of the $1.00 top picture palaces playing one of those present day music scores, with its arrangement for ten violins and a theme strain which haunts the memory for days because of its

---

* *When the epic film* The Queen of Sheba *(starring Betty Blythe and directed by J. Gordon Edwards in 1921) had a local screening in Liverpool, England, shortly after its release, the half dozen men in the pit were led by Jim McCartney—father of Paul McCartney of the Beatles—who claims they didn't know what to play for the film, being called in only for this special occasion. For the chariot race they chose "Thanks for the Buggy Ride," and for the Queen's death, a popular number, "Horsey Keep Your Tail Up." (Reported in Hunter Davies'* The Beatles, the Authorized Biography, *N.Y. McGraw-Hill, 1968, p. 30.)*

beauty and quality, I am reminded that I was the first perpetrator of so-called special music for the films. Music cues, we called them. They originated at the old Vitagraph Studios in Flatbush, Brooklyn, New York, in the early part of 1910, when I was assistant publicity worker for the late Sam Spedon, dean of all picture press agents.

"Spedon was the editor of the Vitagraph Bulletin, the first moving picture studio house organ. Knowing that I had come from a career of crime in vaudeville and Tin Pan Alley, the haunt of the music publishers, Sam conceived the idea of having me furnish appropriate musical suggestions for the various Vitagraph releases. Fearing nothing, I undertook the assignment with much enthusiasm and a loyal heart for the numbers of the publishers for whom I had worked and the songs written by my brother, the late Harry Ennis. To further show the ease with which I could supply musical settings for the movies turned out by Blackton, Rock and Smith, I didn't bother to view the various films. I simply scanned one of Sam Spedon's synopses of the current flicker, sat down at the typewriter, and with the aid of a good memory, plus the catalogues of Remick, Feist, Von Tilzer, Ted Snyder, Witmark, etc., proceeded to cue the film for the benefit of the piano player and three piece orchestras which were paid by exhibitors in 1910 under the belief that they were assisting the picture with harmony and melody. The piano players who received the Ennis system of Vitagraph Music Cues probably felt after a while that there were only a limited number of musical compositions in the world and that Remick and his fellow publishers had the exclusive rights to these compositions. An Irish story, with Leo Deleaney and Maurice Costello in the leading roles, was a cinch for my method of scoring. I suggestted "Has Anybody Here Seen Kelly?," "Mother Machree," "The River Shannon," and "Ireland Must Be Heaven for My Mother Came From There." Tear jerkers, as ballads of a sentimental nature were called in published parlance in those days, received a heavy play in the Vitagraph Music Cues. "My Gal Sal," "I'm Tying the Leaves So They Won't Fall Down," "Let Me Be Your Little Girl," "A Bird in a Gilded Cage," "The Mansion of Aching Hearts," and similar tear pullers were scored time and again for the Vitagraphs which carried the heart throbs and pathos, as enacted by Florence Turner, Earl Williams and Harry Morey. When a war picture came along the music cues wrote themselves, "The Blue and the Grey," "Mama's Boy," "Good Bye, Dolly Gray," "Break the News to Mother," "Good Bye, Little Girl, Good Bye," and numerous other soldier songs did yeoman duty, whether the film was that of the Civil or Spanish war period. We played no favorites. We showed our class by injecting at times the classical and standard numbers—a few of them, anyhow. "Hearts and Flowers," "Melody in F," "Träumerei," "Souvenir," "Pilgrims' Chorus,"—they all helped to give helpless audiences a barrage of highbrow music before the present day experts in the writing of music scores for films discovered Debussy, Beethoven, Schubert, Mozart, Wagner and other big leaguers of the classical field. Jack Fuld, now an exploiter for Metro Goldwyn and then a piano player in a nickelodeon in Bay Ridge, was a steady customer for our music cues. I think Jack still believes we were paid by the publishers of popular music to plug their songs in the Vitagraph Bulletin. But it's not so, Jack. We didn't think of it at the time. Good or bad, these suggestion for musical accompaniment were the trail blazers for the important part that proper scoring plays today in the presentation of every big time film in many movie houses." (From a manuscript in the files of the Department of Film, Museum of Modern Art, New York.)

The Edison Company had sent out musical suggestion sheets the year before Ennis claims he began this service for Vitagraph. In 1909 these *suggestions for music* were part of Edison's booking service. This seems to be the earliest indication of cue sheets, which theatre musicians used thereafter until the advent of sound films. Max Winkler, in his autobiography, *A Penny from Heaven,* [*] writes about his "invention of the musical cue sheet" in 1912. It is assumed that many persons and many film companies started these musical ideas simultaneously, an innovation that gradually developed impressive, original scores.

A typical and unique example from the Edison Company is their musical suggestion sheet for *Frankenstein*, 1910, released as production 287. The film, in one reel, 975 feet, was a "liberal adaptation of Mrs. Shelley's famous story, made to carefully eliminate all the actually repulsive situations, and to concentrate its endeavors upon the mystic and psychological problems that are to be found in this weird tale," comprising twenty-five scenes.

At opening
    Andante — "Then You'll Remember Me"

Till Frankenstein's laboratory
    Moderato — "Melody in F"

Till monster is forming
    Increasing agitato

Till monster appears over bed
    Dramatic music from "Der Freischütz"

Till father and girl in sitting room
    Moderato

Till Frankenstein returns home
    Andante — "Annie Laurie"

Till monster enters Frankenstein's sitting room
    Dramatic — "Der Freischütz"

Till girl enters with teapot
    Andante — "Annie Laurie"

Till monster comes from behind curtain
    Dramatic — "Der Freischütz"

Till wedding guests are leaving
    Bridal Chorus from "Lohengrin"

Till monster appears
    Dramatic — "Der Freischütz"

The EDISON
KINETOGRA

VOL. 2   MARCH 15, 1910

SCENE FROM
FRANKENSTEIN
FILM No. 6604

EDISON FILMS RELEASED F
MARCH 16 TO 31 INCLU

[*] *Published by Appleton-Century-Crofts, 1951. An excerpt appears in* Films in Review, *v. 2, no. 10, December 1951, pp. 34-42.*

Till Frankenstein enters
    Agitato

Till monster appears
    Dramatic — "Der Freischütz"

Till monster vanishes in mirror
    Diminishing Agitato

This was sketchy, unimaginative, but probably helpful to the pianist in those early days. Compare such a suggestion sheet with those that were circulated with films a decade or two later.

The musical director of a theatre in Albany, Georgia, contributed a partial cue sheet of his own selections for a showing of *Judith of Bethulia* in 1914[*] (Reel 2)—

Assyrians storm walls
    Storm scene and last Allegro from *William Tell* Overture.
Hawkes' melodramatic music Nos. 11 and 12, until "Yet Holofernes Took
    Council."
Rosamund Overture (andante) until "Vision Came from the Lord."
Melody of Peace (by Carroll) until "She Put on Garments of Gladness."
Romantic Overture (allegro).

or for the final reel of the film —
Vision of Salome until "Let Me Be Thine Handmaid."
Apache Waltz (Offenbach). *Sunshine and Showers* overture.
King Mydas overture until "Runs Out to Battle."
Light Cavalry overture until prayer by inhabitants.
Christmas Song until joyfulness.
Priests' March—Athalia until end of reel.

Blanche Sweet and Henry B. Walthall in Griffith's **Judith of Bethulia** (1914). Historians have reported that this is the first film where musicians played on the set during production to put the actors in the proper mood. Blanche Sweet says she does not remember it, but that there was music-making during the filming of several of her pictures.

[*] *George P. Montgomery in* Moving Picture World, *July 11, 1914, p. 292. Mr. Montgomery claimed to have used more than twenty musical numbers for one day's pictures of three reels.*

Here is another example of musical cueing, as reported by Clarence E. Sinn in *Moving Picture World*[*]—

"Our old friend, Will H. Bryant, writes: 'I have moved from Indianapolis to this city (Terre Haute, Ind.), and have been managing the house and leading the orchestra since June 3. Am enclosing my program for the Sarah Bernhardt film *Camille*. The manager of these pictures was good enough to ask for a list, saying it fit the picture better than any yet found. Hope it may be of use.'

Camille

1. *Waltz lento* until Camille and Armand alone, then,
2. 'The Flatterer (Chaminade) twice through.
3. 'Scarf Dance.
4. 'Serenade (Puerner) or 'Spring Song' (Mendelssohn).

Second Act

5. 'Confidence (Mendelssohn). Twice.
6. 'Berceuse (Godard) or *Waltz lento* until:
       Camille's Home in the Country
7. 'Evening Star (*Tannhäuser*), until Armand's father leaves Camille.
8. 'Calm as the Night (Bohm), until next title.
9. 'Song without Words (Tchaikovsky). To end of act. Tempo according to action.
10. 'La Bohème Fantasie (Puccini), until Camille out of bed.
11. 'Barcarolle (*Tales of Hoffmann*), until Camille's arm drops to her side.
12. 'Ase's Death (*Peer Gynt Suite* — Grieg), until end . . ."

* *August 31, 1912, p. 871.*

Incidental Music
to

THE THIEF OF BAGDAD

MORTIMER WILSON
Opus 74

The music for many of Douglas Fairbank's spectacular costume films was written and arranged by Mortimer Wilson and scored for full orchestra. Wilson's music for **The Thief of Bagdad** (1924) is one of the best scorings for a silent film.

Shown here also are excerpts (piano arrangement) from the original manuscript of the score for **The Black Pirate** (1926).

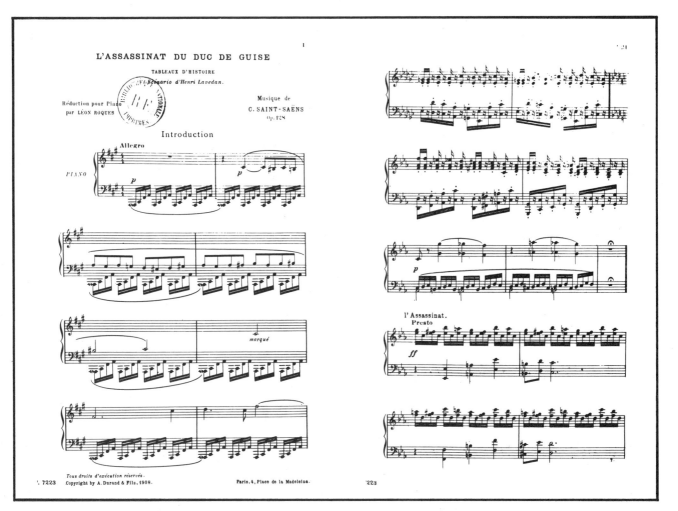

In 1907 distinguished composer Camille Saint-Saens wrote a score especially for the production of Film D'Art, Paris—**L'Assassinet du Duc de Guise.** The score was the very first written especially for a film. Saint-Saens scored it for strings, piano and harmonium and published it as Opus 128. An introduction and five tableaux are musically cued to each scene. The film was less than ten minutes in length. The only "cue" was on page 21 of the score—"l'Assassinet" (Presto)—and corresponds to the photograph shown here.

(Piano score courtesy A. Durand et Fils, Paris, and Elkan-Vogel Co., Philadelphia)

"Turn to any of the 674 pages for any mood you need." Erno Rapee compiled a gigantic volume—*Motion Picture Moods for Pianists and Organists, a Rapid Reference Collection of Selected Pieces Adapted to Fifty-Two Moods and Situations*. It was brought out in 1924 and was probably God-sent for many movie house musicians who had to arrange musical scores for perhaps two or three different feature films a week. This compilation was probably used in hundreds of movie houses across America in theatres that had no large libraries and depended on cue sheets or arranged scores that accompanied many films.

Erno Rapee prefaced the volume by explaining that he "tried to create the necessary bridge between the screen and the audience which is created in the larger motion picture houses by the orchestra.

"If we consider that the theatres of the size and standard of the Capitol Theatre in New York have half a dozen or so musical experts under the direction of the Musical Director working out the music to fit the action to the screen, we realize what a very hard task it must be for any single individual, either at the piano or the organ, to go through with music selected at random and generally at very short notice, and supply good musical accompaniment to pictures. . . . This collection is meant to do away with the aforesaid haphazard collection of music and its use for synchronizing pictures. Inasmuch as most pianists or organists in the smaller theatres do not get a chance, or a very poor one, to review the pictures before the public performance, you can readily see the difficulty under which they work with quickly changing scenes, different psychological situations chasing each other, back-shots, close-ups, close-ins, etc., etc. In creating fifty-two divisions and classifications in this Manual, I tried to give the most numbers to those classes of music which are most frequently called upon to synchronize actions on the screen. . . . You can't always portray action; one-third of all film footage is used to depict action; another third will show no physical action, but will have, as a preponderance, psychological situations; the remaining third will . . . restrict itself to showing or creating atmosphere or scenery. . . ."

EISENSTEIN'S "POTEMKIN" — MUSIC BY EDMUND MEISEL

Director Eisenstein writes—*Potemkin*—at least in its foreign circulation —had a special score written for it. . . . Less usual, perhaps, was the way the score was composed. It was written very much as we work today on a sound-track. Or rather, *as we should always work,* with creative friendship and friendly creative collaboration between composer and director. . . . So it was *Potemkin* . . .

stylistically broke away from the limits of the 'silent film with musical illustration' into a new sphere—into *sound-film,* where true models of this art-form live in a unity of fused musical and visual images, composing the work with a united audio-visual image. . . ." (More details are found in Eisenstein's *Film Form,* pp. 177-178, whence comes this quotation.) (New York, Harcourt, Brace & Co., 1949; reprinted by Meridian Books, 1957.)

"For the New York presentation of *Potemkin* at the Biltmore the original accompanying score by Dr. Edmund Meisel, of Berlin, was used. Of the film itself, one need say little here. It has made cinema history already. The music was almost passed over entirely by the critics of the metropolitan press, which was a mistake, for the score is as powerful, as vital, as galvanic and electrifying as the film. It is written in the extreme modern vein, cacophonies run riot, harmonies grate, crackle, jar; there are abrupt changes and shifts in the rhythm; tremendous chords crashing down, dizzy flights of runs, snatches of half-forgotten melodies, fragments, a short interpolation of jazz on a piano and a melody in the central portion of the film when the people of Odessa stand on the steps waving to the sailors on the cruiser Potemkin and others go out on fishing boats with provisions for them—that is one of the loveliest I have ever heard. It sings! It soars and endears itself to the heart. It is full of gratitude and the love of man for man. It is one of the warmest, tenderest passages that has found its way into the cinema-music repertoire." HERMAN G. WEINBERG, *New York Herald Tribune,* April 29, 1928

Eisenstein's **Potemkin**—Music by Edmund Meisel
Photocopy of the first page sent by Jay Leyda from East Berlin where the orchestral parts were discovered recently. The excerpt shows "the start of the trombone part . . . it does state two of the score's main themes. There is no conducting score yet found." (Letter to Eileen Bowser when the photocopy was sent to Charles Hofmann.)

Piano score for Eisenstein's **October (Ten Days That Shook the World)** composed by Edmund Meisel (1928). Dance sequence.

(Sent by Jay Leyda)

Die Geschichte des Prinzen Achmed (The Adventures of Prince Achmed) was the work of the silhouette artist Lotte Reiniger, and is the first feature length animated film. It was produced in Germany between 1923 and 1926.

The musical score was by Wolfgang Zeller, who inserted 93 picture frames to be used as cues. The atmosphere of this Oriental fantasy was enhanced by Zeller's music. A first performance of this work in this country was heard in 1930 when Arthur Fiedler conducted the Boston Symphony Orchestra during a screening at one of the orchestra's concerts.

The final page of the piano score is shown here with silhouette pictures.

Many theatres installed disc record equipment with double turntables in order to have continuous music pre-recorded. Specific cueing was important and a cue sheet was made up, timed to the film, using standard music available on commercial discs.

An example of this is found in the record scoring for *The Adventures of Prince Achmed.* The beginning of the turntable cue sheet is as follows —

Cue	Start position	Name*
Main Title (at screening)	Beginning	*Daphnis and Chloe*, Pt. 1 (Ravel)
Title: "Great was the might of the African Sorcerer . . ."	Beginning	*L'Apprenti Sorcier*, Pt. 1 (Dukas)
Title: "Far and wide . . ."	1 in. from beginning	*Love for Three Oranges*, Pt. 1 (Prokofieff)
Scene: Magic horse followed by Sorcerer	Beginning	*L'Apprenti Sorcier*, Pt. 1
Scene: Birds in air (yellow) — just after 2nd scene of Sorcerer bowed down before Caliph	About center	*The Fire Bird*, Pt. 3 (Stravinsky)
Title: "East of the sun . . ."	Beginning	*Bena Mora*, Pt. 1 (Holst)
Title: "On a neighboring island . . ."	1 in. from beginning	*The Fire Bird*, Pt. 4
Scene: Achmed beginning to chase Peri Banu	Beginning	*L'Isle Joyeuse* (Debussy)
Title: "After journeying many miles the horse descended"	1 in. from beginning	*The Fire Bird*, Pt. 4

etc.

* *The Part numbers indicate record side of 78 rpm disc albums. This is much easier for cueing than from lp microgroove discs, and more accurate than pre-recorded tape which speeds vary and never synchronize with specific scenes. This is partly due to the fact that in using pre-recorded tapes the speeds do not vary with the running speed of projectors, many of which do not have variable speeds. Optical or magnetic sound tracks on film is the only satisfactory synchronization.*

In November 1967 the Museum of Modern Art held a retrospective of the films of Fritz Lang. Most of these were silent and I furnished my own original piano accompaniments for them. I received a letter and inscribed photograph from Fritz Lang who wrote "Thanking you for your fine accompaniment of *Spies* and in appreciation of your sympathy for my films. . . ."

Outstanding musical scores have been written through the years for Lang's silent films. Most of them are now lost. Gottfried Huppertz composed the music for the two films of *Die Nibelungen* (1923-1924)—*Siegfried* and *Kriemhilds Rache* (Kriemhild's Revenge)—but which was (as Lang writes) "replaced by Mr. Hitler of unholy memory by music of Richard Wagner."[*] Hupperts also composed the score for *Metropolis* (1926). Werner Richard Heymann is the composer for *Spione* (Spies) (1928), while Willy Schmidt Gentner contributed the accompaniment for *Frau Im Mond* (Woman in the Moon) (1929).

[*] *Letter to the author, April 16, 1968.*

COMES STRAVINSKY TO THE FILM THEATRE

"... Properly, the American premier of *The Cabinet of Dr. Caligari* employed music calculated to heighten its exotic character, to underline its fantastic aspects. At the Capitol Theater, where the film was introduced, the admirable symphony orchestra played a special score arranged from the writings of the modernists Debussy, Strauss, Stravinsky and others. Of the compiling and adapting of the music let S. L. Rothafel—in charge of the artistic destinies of the big theater—speak.

'In handling the musical problem presented by *The Cabinet of Dr. Caligari* Mr. Rapee and I felt that the orthodox thing would not do. A film conceived along revolutionary lines called for a score faithfully synchronized in mood and development. We took psychology into reckoning—the psychology of the audience no less than of the play. In the phantasmagorical scheme of *Dr. Caligari* people move and live in a world out of joint. The cracked country is dotted with grotesque houses, skinny twisted trees, enormously steep and rutted pathways. . . . The key principle of this sprawling architecture and wild terrain is distortion. With that steadily in mind we built up the score. We went to Schönberg, Debussy, Stravinsky, Prokofieff, Richard Strauss for the thematic material. We assembled our themes, assigned characteristic ideas to the principals of the play, and then proceeded to distort the music. The music had, as it were, to be made eligible for citizenship in a nightmare country.

The Cabinet of Dr. Caligari (1919), directed by Robert Wiene. Werner Krauss in the title role, with Conrad Veidt as Cesare the Somnambulist, and Lil Dagover as Jane.

'The score is built up on the leitmotif system; quite in the Wagnerian manner. For Caligari's motif we went to Strauss' *Till Eulenspiegel*. His idea recurs, or is suggested whenever Caligari or his influence is at work on the screen. To identify Cesare, the somnambulist, Mr. Rapee and I borrowed a bit from Debussy's *Afternoon of a Faun*. These main ideas appear singly or together, whole or in part, as the psychology of the tale demands. The scoring is not that of the original, but has been done here and is contrived to emphasize the macabre. Muted brass was resorted to for most of the sinister sounds.

'I think I may confidently, and justly, say that the whole represents the most daring musical achievement in the history of the American motion-picture theater. We tried very hard with this picture, because we think so much of it. *Caligari* is, to my mind, an imaginative masterpiece and a triumph of directing. Musically no less than pictorially it opens up a virgin country.'

"As briefly back as five years Stravinsky or Schönberg in the movie-house belonged to the inconceivable. Today it calmly happens, and the audience calmly swallows the pill. It would have been far simpler, in preparing accompaniment for this film, to dish up the old safe and sickening potpourri. The more admirable, then, is the departure made by Messrs. Rothafel and Rapee. The thing took more than courage; it meant double labor and it meant considerable expense. Four rehearsals were called. But the tune was worth the toll. The acrid air of Stravinsky has been borne into the film theater. It may clear the sweet murk before the last reel is run."

B. R., in *Musical America*,
April 16, 1921

Photograph of the "Grand Orchestra" inscribed for David Mendoza, 1926.

"Having listened to many symphony concerts in the past several weeks it was particularly interesting to gauge the work of David Mendoza and his orchestra at the Capitol Theatre and to compare the musical effectiveness of that organization with the more classical ones that are appearing weekly in Carnegie Hall, Mecca Auditorium,* and in the Metropolitan Opera House. There is a strong point in common. I have conceded recently that whatever overtures or selection the Capitol Theatre orchestra sets out to play, a fine sense of dignity and *esprit de corps* is at once apparent.

* *Now the New York City Center.*

PROGRAM
Week Beginning Sunday, December 5th, 1926

MAJOR EDWARD BOWES
Managing Director, Capitol Theatre, takes pleasure in offering
the following entertainment:
Created, Lighted and Staged Under His Personal Direction

---

1. CAPITOL GRAND ORCHESTRA
DAVID MENDOZA, Conductor
Eugene Ormandy, Associate Conductor
Waldo Mayo, Concertmaster   Yasha Bunchuk, Solo Cellist
Maurice Baron, Orchestration
COMPOSITION AND ARRANGEMENT—DR. WILLIAM AXT
Max Herzberg, Assistant to Dr. Axt
H. C. Frommel, Librarian
SELECTIONS FROM "FAUST" .... Gounod
NOTE—This opera, based on the well-known tragedy by Goethe,
was first produced in Paris in 1859. Since then it has marched
triumphantly over all lyric stages of the world, and it is
claimed that even today "Faust" is sung more than any other
opera.. The selections which we present this week comprise
the finest gems of the work.
(Presented at 2:00, 4:00, 7:30, 9:30)

2. RUDY WIEDOEFT, Saxophone Virtuoso
(a) "Melodie" .... General Charles G. Dawes
(b) "Valse Mazanetta" .... Wiedoeft
(c) "Sax-ema" .... Wiedoeft
(d "Land of the Sky Blue Water" .... Cadman
(Presented at 2:10, 4:10, 7:40, 9:40)

3. CAPITOL MAGAZINE
An institutional compilation of pictorial news of the week edited
from a standpoint of entertainment and
psychological arrangement of its salient fea
is called to the musical arrangement and
(Presented at 12:32, 2:16, 4:16, 5:

4. CELIA TURRILL, Mezzo Sopra
"Flower Song" from "Faust"
(Presented at 2:25, 4:25, 7:

5. BALLET from "FAUST"—"WALPURGIS NIGHT"
CAST
Mephistopheles .... John Triesault
Faust .... Rita Glynde
Mercury .... Roland Guerard
The Dancer .... Joyce Coles
CAPITOL BALLET CORPS: Pavla Reiser, Claire Dearfield,
Ruth Southgate, Connie Polsley, Ruth Alpert, Eva Hellesnes
CHESTER HALE GIRLS: Mary Hiscox, Elsie Duffy,
Ruby McDonald, Lillian Messmer, Jean Walton, Clara Fay,
Rolande Poucel, Anna Folwasny, Violette Lundberg,
Jeanne Kroll, Kiki Talas, Etta Moore, Mary Wynn,
Jewel Tiedgens, Gladys Glorita, Julie Guelofiantz
(a) "Waltz" .... Capitol Ballet Corps
(b) "Slave Dance" .... Mr. Guerard
(c) "Bacchante" .... Miss Coles
(d) "Bacchanal"
Principals, Capitol Ballet Corps and Chester Hale Girls
(Presented at 2:30, 4:30, 8:00, 10:00)

6.

GOETHE'S
"FAUST"
With EMIL JANNINGS
THE CAST

Cherub .... Warner Fuetterer
The Evil Spirit, Called Mephisto ...... Emil Jannings
Faust .... Gosta Ekman
Marguerite .... Camilla Horn
Her Mother .... Frieda Richard
Her Brother Valentine .... Wilhelm Dieterle
Her Aunt Martha .... Yvette Guilbert
The Duke .... Eric Barclay
The Duchess .... Hanna Ralph

Directed by F. W. MURNAU
An UFA PRODUCTION
A METRO-GOLDWYN-MAYER PICTURE
(Presented at 12:41, 2:38, 4:38, 6:07, 8:08, 10:08)

7. CAPITOL GRAND ORGAN
DR. MELCHIORRE MAURO-COTTONE, Chief Organist
CARL McKINLEY, Associate Organist
NOTE:—The program is subject to change at any time without
notice, and the foregoing time schedule is approximate and
intended merely for the guidance of our patrons.
Choreography by Chester Hale, Balle: Master
Settings by Arthur Knorr—Art Director

"CHRISTMAS CARDS AND PARCELS—
SHOP EARLY AND MAIL EARLY FOR
DELIVERY BEFORE CHRISTMAS"

Chester Hale, director of the Capitol Theatre Ballet
School holds classes every afternoon at 5:00 P.M. Appli-
cants for admission to the school may apply at the stage
door on Saturday mornings at 10:00. Pupils must be
Sixteen years or over. There is no tuition charge.

Estey Organ Company, Designers and Builders of the Capitol Organ
Lyon and Healy Harp Used   Brunswick Phonograph Used
The Steinway is the Official Piano of the Capitol
Floral Decorations by Warendorff
Emergency Room on Grand Mezzanine
Trained Nurses in Charge: Mary Griffin and Katherine Sheridan
Staff Chiropodist—Dr. Max Nachbar

For the convenience of our patrons we have installed an
Umbrella Service. There is no charge for this accommoda-
tion. Patrons are requested to leave a deposit of $1.00
which will be refunded upon return of the umbrella.

Major Edward Bowes and his Capitol Family broadcast
every Sunday night from 7:20 to 9:15 from stations
WEAF, New York; WRC, Washington; WJAR, Provi-
dence; WWI, Detroit; WCAE, Pittsburgh; WEEI, Boston;
WTAG, Worcester; and KSD, St. Louis, by courtesy of
the National Broadcasting Company (Incorporated).

Program of the Capitol Theater, New York City, with the "Grand Orchestra" conducted by David Mendoza. Associate conductor was Eugene Ormandy. The program was distributed for the week of December 5, 1926, when the feature attraction was Murnau's **Faust**. Most of the elaborate program which served as a curtain-raiser was devoted to the music from Gounod's opera.

"Always a firm believer and ardent booster of fine music when it is finely done—as well as a ruthless critic of indifferent, inexpert and carelessly played motion picture music—no doubt I am inclined to lean over backward in encouraging this interesting American art-form, but David Mendoza and his orchestra need little push from my pen, as they are apparently now headed.

"There is no orchestra similar to this one in our country, as far as my travels have led me, and certainly nothing comparable to it in Paris, Berlin, Rome or London picture palaces."

THEODORE STEARNS, Music Critic
Morning Telegraph, New York
Reprinted in Capitol Theatre program,
Week beginning December 5, 1926

The opening music for the film which served as a curtain-raiser before the main title.

"*The Big Parade* represents the supreme catharsis in the field of synchronization. The accompanying score of Messrs. Mendoza and Axt to Vidor's film was more than a mere accompaniment—it was a sheer triumph of mind over matter. It so completely transcended everything that has preceded it that its power to stir us to the point of pain was accepted without surprise—so engrossed were we in the cinema-bewitchment, so completely had we forgotten the presence of the camera, of a specially prepared orchestra and the artificialities of a theater.

Tom O'Brien, John Gilbert and Karl Dane in a tense scene before the signal for "over the top."

"... The score utilized popular army songs ... paraphrasing them in a hundred different ways, with turns that whipped the blood. Following the fearful racket of the sirens announcing the declaration of war, the music begins to get troubled and by its very studied calmness rises into mild hysteria to the point where Jim (John Gilbert) confesses that he's enlisted—break—diminuendo. A perfect first sequence. ..."

HERMAN G. WEINBERG,
New York Herald Tribune,
April 29, 1928

Theme from **Don Juan,** the first Vitaphone feature film, 1926, directed by Alan Crosland, with John Barrymore, Mary Astor, and Myrna Loy. The musical score for this Warner's feature was composed and arranged by David Mendoza and William Axt. The fragment from Mendoza was inscribed to the author in 1969—". . . whose remarkable memory recalled to me many nostalgic hours of great musical experiences."

"I WANT CHAPLIN-TYPE MUSIC HERE"

A Hollywood director explains this to his composer. Through his many decades in films, Chaplin contributed complementary music as backgrounds to enhance his moods. As writer, director, star, producer, Chaplin also was composer. Theodore Huff writes about *Chaplin as Composer—*

When *City Lights* first appeared in 1931 with the credit-title "Music composed by Charles Chaplin," there was a surprised and indulgent raising of eyebrows. Because musically-minded people recognized here and there a phrase of some well known melody (usually inserted for comic effect), and because "La Violetera" ("Who'll Buy My Violets"), the song made famous by Raquel Meller on her 1926 tour of the U.S. was used as a theme for the blind girl, they assumed that Chaplin was stretching it a bit in order that the public be certain that from him came everything in the film. However, with the subsequent appearances of *Modern Times* (again with a complete original score—except for "Titina"), *The Great Dictator* and *Monsieur Verdoux* (both talkies with occasional interludes and "background" music), and with the reissued *The Gold Rush* (also with continuous accompaniment), some of the same doubters began to realize that from the music for these five pictures, although arranged and orchestrated by various others, emanates a flavor which can only be described as "Chaplinesque." Those who still believe that Chaplin merely hummed a tune or two and that "real musicians" did the rest have only to listen to the musical scores of more than one of his films. The signs of Chaplin's characteristic style cannot be easily missed— among them his particular fondness for romantic waltz hesitations played in very rubato time, for lively numbers in 2/4 time which might be called promenade themes, and for rhythmic tangos.

Chaplin's music is an integral part of his conception of the film, and though D. W. Griffith similarly composed some of the themes for his pictures, it can be said of Chaplin that he is virtually unique in that no other one man ever before had written, directed, acted, *and scored* a motion picture. Incidentally, Chaplin even insists on conducting the orchestra during recording. Perhaps this is one reason for the satisfying wholeness of Chaplin films.

Though untrained in music, Chaplin inherited his natural talent from his father who was a music-hall singer of considerable fame and from his mother who sang in Gilbert and Sullivan operettas.

Realizing the importance of proper musical accompaniment to the silent film, Chaplin supervised the cue sheets (lists of numbers to be played, sent free to all theatres booking a film) of his pictures from *The Kid* (1921) to *City Lights* (1931) when it was possible to have the music on the film itself reproduced in every theatre exactly as he wished it. Also it was a commercial expedient to claim at least "music and sound effects" for by 1931 the silent picture had been entirely superseded by the "talkie."

While it is true that Arthur Johnston and Alfred Newman arranged and orchestrated the music for *City Lights,* the fact remains that all the melodies, with the above exceptions noted, are compositions by Chaplin. There are at least twenty distinct numbers, which could be published apart from the content of the film. As was customary with scoring for silent pictures, the Wagnerian *leitmotif*

Scene from **The Vagabond** (1916) in which Chaplin played the violin as a tramp-musician.

system was employed, and a musical theme associated with each character and idea. There are about 95 main cues in *City Lights,* not counting those passages where the music follows the action closely in what is generally known as "mickey-mousing," the technique favored in the scoring of animated cartoons.

Considered strictly from a composer's standpoint Chaplin's music cannot be classified with such modern motion picture scores as those of Virgil Thomson, Max Steiner, Miklos Rozsa or William Walton. Thomson's scoring for *The River* and *Louisiana Story,* with extremely clever arrangements of old folk tunes, is far more sophisticated and intellectual. Nor does Chaplin possess the special virtuosity and present grandiose manner of Steiner where too often sheer bombast attempts to compensate for the emotional vacuity in the picture itself. But who other than Chaplin could more brilliantly and meaningfully support with music the tragic-comic adventures of the tramp character he himself created?

Published music and recordings are attributed to Chaplin the composer. In **The Chaplin Revue** he drew upon the mood of the twenties for his themes, the period in which the films were made. Not only does the music so aptly suit the pictures, but on hearing it we can actually see the tramp being chased by cops, evading thieves, drilling in the army and giving a sermon (of David and Goliath) in church as the Pilgrim. (Decca disc 4040)

For the first Vitaphone attraction in 1926 a theme from William Axt and David Mendoza's score for **Don Juan** was adapted as a song to exploit the film with words by Harry Lee to be sung by Metropolitan Opera star Anna Case. Arthur A. Penn's **Smilin' Through** had been featured during the stage play, later for Norma Talmadge's production, Norma Shearer's production, and then sung in the sound version by Jeanette MacDonald.

"Theme songs" were associated with many films during the final years of the silent era and almost every major production had its especially composed song. These songs were not only heard as background music during the films, but were used to advertise and exploit the feature. Sheet music and recordings were released prior to the film showings. Several stars recorded these songs and made personal appearances to sing them as curtain raisers.

Erno Rapee's score for *What Price Glory?* (1926) contained his song *Charmaine*, with words by Lew Pollack, who later collaborated on the love waltz *Diane* for *Seventh Heaven* (1927). A title song was written for Dolores Del Rio's *Ramona* the same year and she recorded it. Sheet music of such songs flooded the market, together with recordings, especially with the coming of the sound film. Most of these films were musicals—"all talking, all singing, all dancing."

Almost from the beginning the movies were a good subject for songs which became popular. One would hear such ditties as "Take Your Girl to the Movies If You Can't Make Love at Home," or "What Will We Do On Saturday Night

Now That the Town's Gone Dry?" (The movies, of course.)

Through the years songs have been dedicated to movie stars. Fatty Arbuckle, Mabel Normand, Charlie Chaplin, Mary Pickford had their photographs on song covers. Louis Gottschalk's theme from his score for Griffith's *Broken Blossoms* was published as a song called *White Blossoms* and dedicated to Lillian Gish.

For years during production of films, musicians were employed to be on the set during shooting to promote varying moods for the actors during specific scenes. A piano, portable organ, violin and cello were part of every studio's equipment.

Many stars who worked in early films have stories about on-the-set musicians. Many directors realized the value of music during filming, or between takes. Some directors would never have music while filming.

Blanche Sweet says, "There was music, and it seemed to help everyone from the stars to the technicians, stage hands, carpenters, electricians, everybody.

For some films there were always musicians . . . but most of the music was between takes, for relaxation, a kind of morale booster. It pepped up everbody. There is one bit of music that will always make me cry: I could cry over a piece of chicken if they played *La Bohème!* I have heard the opera all my life and would cry if you played it for me now! Griffith never used any music while he was filming that I remember. He always said that he would never employ actors who could not feel the role enough to weep at rehearsals. Therefore he said nobody needed music to create the right mood. When the scene was right, the take was good, Griffith always said, 'It sings!' I do remember music for a film we made in 1924 called *Those Who Dance.* Thomas Ince, the producer, had music on the set, and Bessie Love and I played ukeleles. It was a suspense picture about the illicit liquor traffic, but there were light moments. I will send you a picture of me playing the ukelele to prove it!"*

Neil Hamilton wrote his memories on the subject—** "During my four years of extra work from 1918 to 1922 I remember music being played on every set, and on one of them it was a *full* orchestra. I worked on the movie that the great Caruso made. It was at Fort Lee, New Jersey, and he walked all around the studio singing at the top of his voice . . . but the picture was a silent and no one heard but just the gang on the set.

"In 1922 I started with Mr. Griffith out at Mamaroneck, New York, and was with him for almost three years, and strange to say, I have no recollection of any music being played on any of our sets. To listen to the man's voice was music enough! He talked to you through most of the scenes, 'specially the close ups, and it wasn't until I joined Paramount in 1925 and came out to Hollywood that I remember music being on every stage, and I found it very helpful. Soft and lovely during the love scenes and away-to-the-races during the exciting moments, when one went to the front door expecting to see Grandma, only to find Erich Von Stroheim!

"During the shooting of *Beau Geste,* Mr. Brennon had a bugler on the set for me. You may remember the Viking's Funeral that Digby (me) gave to his brother Beau (Ronnie). It was a lovely moment, and during it Digby raised his bugle and blew Taps. Mr. Brennon, the director—and a fine one he was—had me take the instrument out of its holder, do a big flourish before putting it to my lips, and then I blew Taps. But—just in case I might blow too long, and perhaps not long enough so that everyone in the audience would say—'That guy didn't blow Taps. He blew *My Old Kentucky Home,* etc., etc.' The minute I put the mouthpiece to my lips the off-stage bugler began to blow, and I blew along with him so that when the little piece was correctly intoned he quit, and so did I—to the second. Now when we saw the picture for the first time at the old Criterion . . . and when the scene came on the screen, the bugler in the theatre orchestra stood and blew Taps along with me on the screen and when he'd finished the entire house broke into applause. I was thrilled, the moment was so real, and I remember thinking 'Gee! Wouldn't it be wonderful if someday, somehow, they managed to produce sound on the screen!'—without realizing that it was just around the corner!

* *Blanche Sweet in conversation with the author, December 1968.*
** *Neil Hamilton in letter to the author, December 17, 1968.*

"Curiously enough when sound finally arrived, it was the musicians who were hurt most. There just was no work for them. They couldn't play while any rehearsals were going on, and they certainly couldn't play while any cameras were turning, and they were just through, finished, out! There must have been a small army of them, as Hollywood had many studios, made many pictures, as opposed to the inroads these days with foreign productions.

"I remember the fine and thrilling orchestras at the old Strand, the Capitol, the Rivoli and the Paramount. When they were finished playing, the stage would sink down out of sight!"

The movie house organ has been called a "gaudy giant among musical instruments" and flourished for more than a decade in most of the theatres of America. There were many sizes and types from the smallest harmonium to the "mighty Wurlitzer." Most of these organs (heard from World War I until the coming of sound) were glamorous, big, and very versatile. Robert Hope-Jones developed this versatile instrument and called it the "Unit Orchestra." It could do anything with its thousands of pipes, a battery of drums, marimbas, pianos, glockenspiels, xylophones. It could imitate banjos, harpsichords and mandolins. There were sets of bells, cymbals, castanets, tambourines, tom-toms and gongs. The versatility of the organist brought out any effects inspired by the pictures on the screen.

Lillian Gish says, "Griffith would never allow any music on the set. He loved music and had a beautiful, powerful and resonant voice. Often we heard him singing. So many of us loved music so that if it was played as we tried to work we would stop to listen to it and never get the film finished!"[*]

Blanche Sweet plays the ukulele by the swimming pool at the studio between scenes of the filming of **Diplomacy** (1926).

Courtesy of Blanche Sweet

Colleen Moore and her director Alfred E. Green celebrate the completion of **Irene** (1926) with a song. The **Irene** studio orchestra helps out with the music. (Featured song of the film was "Alice Blue Gown" and the film was climaxed with a fashion show.)

Colleen Moore writes—"We always had mood music on the sets. I had a three piece orchestra that played continually, not only to put us in the mood but to amuse us between scenes, since I was making comedies and needed to keep in high spirits. Here I am, showing the orchestra with me. . . . The music really helped the comedy. . . . *Lilac Time* had a memorable score and a beautiful theme song."[**]

[*] *Conversation with the author, October 1968.*
[**] *Colleen Moore in a letter to the author, April 1969.*

Cecil B. DeMille states in his *Autobiography**** that he never wanted music on the set because it interfered with his own mood while trying to direct. Many of his stars demanded it and DeMille would walk about the set with his hands over his ears to keep from hearing it. He felt that if he allowed himself to be influenced by the mood music, his judgment of the acting was likely to be faulty. "Under the spell of the music, I might be deeply moved by the scene, but later, when I ran it on the screen in silence, find it cold and flat. It was not, therefore, a soulless DeMille who rudely covered his ears against the seductive melodies of the mood music . . . it was only the cobbler sticking to his last . . . the director remembering . . . the *story* he is trying to tell."

DeMille early came to the conclusion (which Griffith had already reached independently) that the producer of a film should provide the musical score to go with it so that the accompaniment would help the story and not hurt it.

The distinguished cast of **Beau Geste** (1926) on location in the desert "making music" under director Herbert Brennon's guidance. Ralph Forbes (snaredrum), Ronald Colman (trombone), Noah Beery (organ), Victor McLaglen (cello), Neil Hamilton (trumpet) and William Powell (bugle) are among the orchestra's members. The photo, posed for publicity, does show the instruments which staff musicians used for atmosphere. Score was compiled and synchronized by Hugo Riesenfeld.

D. W. Griffith made some predictions and emphasized his philosophy in 1924 in an article, "The Movies 100 Years From Now," and has this to say about music for the films—

". . . I am quite positive that when a century has passed, all thought of our

* *Englewood Cliffs, N.J., Prentice-Hall, Inc., 1959.*

Two musicians known as Bush and Dolores add to the atmosphere of **The Exquisite Sinner** (1925) when Joseph Von Sternberg brought his star, Paulette Duval, to the Pacific coast beach near Santa Monica. Cameraman was Max Fabian, and Von Sternberg's assistants were Robert Florey and Nick Grinde.

Collection of Herman G. Weinberg.

so-called speaking pictures will have been abandoned. It will never be possible to synchronize the voice with the pictures. This is true because the very nature of the films forgoes not only the necessity for but the propriety of the spoken voice. Music—fine music—will always be the voice of the silent drama. One hundred years from now will find the greatest composers of that day devoting their skill and their genius to the creation of motion-picture music.

"There will be three principal figures in the production of a picture play— the author first, the director and music composer occupying an identical position in importance.

"We do not want now and we never shall want the human voice with our films. Music, as I see it within that hundred years, will be applied to the visualization of the human being's imagination. And, as in your imagination those unseen voices are always perfect and sweet, or else magnificent and thrilling, you will find them registering upon the mind of the picture patron, in terms of lovely music, precisely what the author has intended to be registered there. There is no voice in the world like the voice of music. To me those images on the screen must always be silent. Anything else would work at cross purposes with the real object of this new medium of expression. There will never be speaking pictures. Why should there be when no voice can speak so beautifully as music? There are no dissonant r's and twisted consonants and guttural slurs and nasal twangs in beautiful music. Therefore the average person would much prefer to see his pictures

Gibson Gowland leads his pack mule, his canary in its cage, and his gold into Death Valley for the final scene of Erich von Stroheim's **Greed** (1923). Two musicians play mood music in torrid heat for this realistic drama.

Original score was composed and arranged by Leo Kempenski.

Director Clarence Brown shows Greta Garbo the phonograph he used for atmospheric music out in the woodlands during production of **A Woman of Affairs** (1928). Hobart Bosworth is at the extreme right. Cameraman is William Daniels.

Ernst Lubitsch had a method of playing the piano all his own. Here he takes time off on the set of **The Patriot** (1928) for a solo jam session.

He played the cello too. The fingering and bow arm are accurate. He "picked it up" by himself, as he did the piano.

Photos and caption from Herman G. Weinberg. (**The Lubitsch Touch,** E. P. Dutton, N. Y., 1968, p. 103.)

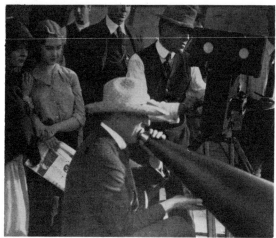

Director D. W. Griffith at the Biograph Studios in New York City, with Billy Bitzer at the camera, Blanche Sweet and Dorothy Gish in the background. This was more than a decade before Griffith's predictions about the future of the films.

and let the voice which speaks to him be the voice of music—one of the most perfect of all the arts.

". . . In the year 2024 we shall have orchestras of many kinds playing for the pictures. Each motion-picture theatre will have several orchestras of diversified character. The big, robust outdoor pictures will have more than one orchestra in attendance at all times. String quartets will play for the mood of a string quarter; sighing guitars and thumpety banjos will play for their mood in the picture play; symphonic orchestras of greater proportions than we now dream of will be employed for moods to fit the sublime and the grand.

"We have scarcely an inkling of what the development of music is going to be in the film play."*

* Collier's, *May 3, 1924, p. 7.*

This is a simple suggestion and any number of ideas can be invented to establish the right music for a film. In most cases, if the themes are strong enough, the audience will recognize them as they appear just as they identify them with the characters of the story.

Some time ago I prepared a new score for Carl Dreyer's *The Passion of Joan of Arc* (1928). Music for the accompaniment of the opening scenes (the main title was missing from the film's print I accompanied) established the drama to come and I include it to illustrate.

Dreyer's film is an intimate one, dealing with the trial and execution of Joan the girl, but very little, if at all, of Joan's past or France's struggle to expel the English. "We see only the faces, the eyes, the tears, the woolen stuffs, leather, steel, stone, sky that (the) camera lingers upon."* Photographs reproduced here illustrate this intimate personal approach which has made Dreyer's film unique. Therefore the music must complement this personal simplicity.

* *Program notes by Iris Barry for the Museum of Modern Art, 19??.*

My accompaniment began with a suggestion of chiming bells, identifed with Joan's spirituality and ecstasy in her belief and purpose. These bells intensify as the film progresses but return to their original effect after Joan's martyrdom and spiritual release. At the beginning after the chimes, the music dissolves into

the rhythm (a sinister motif) of the entrance of the robed judges. At Joan's appearance, there is utter silence. Her simple motif—a folklike tune suitable to her native country village—identifies with her simplicity, especially in comparison

with the judges and their musical motif. The folk tune stumbles and hesitates as Joan herself hesitates in her inarticulate compulsion to supply the right answers which she feels are in her heart. This tune is developed to great intensity as the trial progresses, is heard in menacing minor rhythms during the torture chamber

scenes, and is combined with the judges' theme as she is condemned. It becomes a spiritual hymn, combined with the soft chiming bells, as she meets and faces death as a saint.

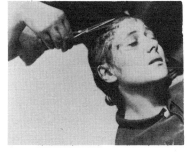

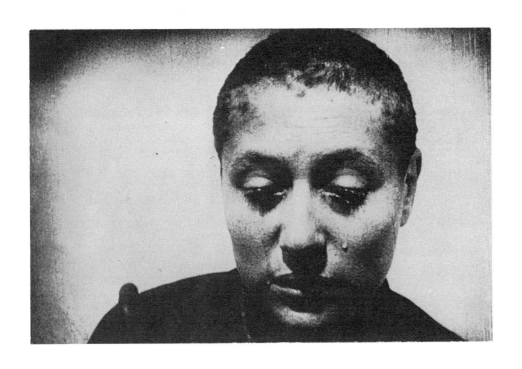

Practically every classic composer of the past has been given a hearing as accompanying music for a film. Beethoven, Schubert, Tchaikovsky and Wagner have been favorites for the movie house arranger.

Arthur Kleiner, accompanist for nearly three decades for screenings at the Museum of Modern Art and who compiled many scores, selected Robert Schumann's music for *Faust* for much of the background during Murnau's *Faust*

(1926) with Emil Jannings. Kleiner's original score for Eisenstein's *Potemkin* was published by the Museum.

Music for "main titles" is very important. Such music sets the mood for the entire film. An atmosphere must be suggested and established; certain themes to be used throughout the film may be introduced; but the *mood* is the most important aspect for the cue—AT SCREENING. The music can make or break the mood of the picture and the right atmosphere must be established musically at the very beginning.

No matter the subject of the film, the accompanist can work out appropriate themes, or *leitmotifs* if you wish, for the characters, the scenes, the situations to follow.

Here is an example.

Constance Talmadge made a number of brilliant comedies, among them *The Duchess of Buffalo* (1926). For the music during its main title I began by suggesting what will follow. The comedy concerned a beautiful dancer from Buffalo, New York, who came to Russia to perform and gathered around her grand dukes and other notables who were soon at her feet. My music began with a suggestion of the Russian National Anthem, overlaid with a familiar American folk tune, "Buffalo Gals, won't you come out tonight and dance by the light of the moon?" The tune was used in various ways during the film, as a waltz, as a love theme, in moments of suspense when the Duchess' intrigues became complicated. The music added to the fun of this charming comedy. Whether or not the audience realized my subtle suggestions in these themes I don't know but there was delight for the accompanist who worked out such ideas.

EARLY FILMS TODAY . . . AND THEIR MUSIC

With the coming of sound films the movie musicians in the pit seemed to disappear. Their place was taken by what was then called "canned music." Some of these musicians found their way into the studios and performed or conducted the synchronized scores adapted to and superimposed on the screen voices.

Since that time these versatile musicians (but infrequently) would be heard when early films were screened and they could again fit the music to the picture as they watched the screen,

Original scores and cue sheets also disappeared with the silent film era, just as many films deteriorated with the years. A few places over the world have made an effort to save this early music, just as films have been preserved and restored in archives.*

With the many hundreds of early films being circulated today to institutions, there is a need for appropriate musical background. Unfortunately, the majority of these films are shown today in silence. At some screenings selected recordings are heard, either discs or tapes. Unfortunately, pre-recorded music seldom synchronizes with the film.

George C. Pratt reports (in letter to the author in January 1969) that there is a collection of film scores at the George Eastman House in Rochester, New York. The collection was made by Theodore Huff and includes the major Griffith scores, various piano scores for such films as *The Big Parade* and *Ben-Hur,* as well as several hundred musical cue sheets and mood pieces, also from Huff.

The Library of Congress Division of Music also reports the inclusion of several important film scores in their collection.

Following the action on the screen and fitting the musical mood with the pictorial is a tricky business. This is why it is best to watch the screen constantly and consistently. This, my own method, is better than watching or following printed musical scores. For the several thousand films that I have accompanied with piano or organ music, I have looked at the *screen only* as the picture changed musical mood; have followed and anticipated always—if possible—to the split second. The musician who uses his imagination, memory and creativeness, has to be an *instant composer.*

The film should be screened as many times as necessary in advance, so that the pianist knows the continuity, can anticipate the action, can plan musical moods, and can organize his materials. There can be both enthusiasm as well as embarrassment when playing for a picture *cold.*

A colleague had been playing piano or small organ in neighborhood theatres, and finally was graduated to a downtown deluxe house that was proud to present a mighty four-manual organ with all the trimmings. My friend was very excited with the possibilities of pulling all the stops and trying all the effects. In her excitement she neglected to screen the film before the audience saw it, and the result was that she "miscued." She was following the film as closely as pos-

---

* *The Museum of Modern Art, as example, has an extensive library of film scores collected during the past three decades. Special scores were also arranged by persons in the department, especially by Arthur Kleiner and Alden Beach. Some of these scores are circulated with the films. A partial listing is included .*

sible and all seemed well. One sequence concerned an old man who was the faithful bell-toller in a church; and in doing his duty he reached up to pull the rope to sound the alarm to alert the village. My friend anticipated, as she thought, and pulled the stop for the effect, and the bells tolled magnificently. A quick sub-title—BUT THE BELLS DID NOT RING!—for the faithful old man had died as he reached for the rope! Audience laughter and an embarrassed organist! Perhaps she learned her lesson after that episode and screened films ahead of time.

Oftentimes prints of films did not arrive at theatres until the day of showing and there was no extra last minute time for prevues. In this case the prepared cue sheets were invaluable and were circulated in advance with publicity materials and press books.

The first film I remember playing for in a theatre (at age sixteen) was at a Saturday afternoon matinee. The program included cartoon, serial, two-reel comedy and Western feature. A variety of music for a beginner! And many moods! Comic fast music, mysterious and dramatic music, and hurry-chase Western allegros as well as a suggestion of cowboy melodies. Except for the cowboy folk-tunes, the afternoon was an improvisation. I decided immediately that this would be my method of interpreting musical backgrounds for all films. I knew it was easier to "catch and hold" the mood in that way until the next scene. Even then I also realized that too familiar music detracted from the visual impact, and that the accompaniment should enhance the visual and stay in the background. I had read an article (and looked it up recently) in *Moving Picture World* written by S. L. Rothapfel ("Roxy" himself) that "pianists must remember that they are merely one of the cogs in the wheel that makes the picture theatre go round, and as a rule, the people pay to *see the picture, not to hear the pianist,* so therefore play softly when occasion demands and always remember *the picture comes first.*"*

The first time I was impressed by music for a film was for *The Birth of a Nation.* (The most discussed film and film musical score of all time!) It was also my first experience with a big orchestra. My age was two and a half and my parents took me to the American Legion Casino in Tampa, Florida, where the picture was screened. I have since seen that epic dozens of times, and will never forget the effects of music with that picture. It was my first hearing of now familiar scores which later I lectured about as music historian.

Since that film is one of the most popular circulated programs today in film societies and institutions, the "method" of supplying musical background for today's audiences should be emphasized. As has been mentioned several times, if the pianist has the talent to improvise there is a great advantage. Music that is too familiar detracts from the enjoyment and tends sometimes to make the film absurd. The audience should never be conscious of a familiar tune. One should realize that the musical background is solely to enhance the visual conception of the film. *The Birth of a Nation* is a good example of what I am trying to point out. Musical backgrounds appropriate in 1915 at the film's premier and original run can not be played today with the same effect—that is, to most audiences—and

* *April 16, 1910. (Originally borrowed from a theatre manager's file, since my first playing for films was in 1929!)*

Henry B. Walthall (Little Colonel) and Lillian Gish (Elsie Stoneman) in final love scene enhanced by Breil's theme.

the whole point lies in the fact that the music is now too familiar, and therefore distracting for today's audiences.

The piano score, credited (as was the orchestration) to selections made by D. W. Griffith, director and creator of the film, in collaboration with Joseph Carl Breil, is 151 pages and represents excerpts from several dozen famous composers' works. In 1915 much of the music of Beethoven, Schubert, Schumann, Weber, Wagner and many others, was unfamiliar to much of the public. Concert going was a rarity in many parts of the United States. Therefore movie audiences felt they were hearing a score especially written for the film. Today all of such music is very familiar.*

Even though Griffith and Breil showed great imagination in compiling the dramatic musical material (it has often been said that Griffith thought of the film "symphonically"), this score cannot be played today in all seriousness except as a "museum piece." Wagner's "Ride of the Valkyries" was used for the Klan ride, music from Grieg's "Peer Gynt" was heard in the scene of the evacuation and burning of Atlanta, and so on. Can you imagine serious performance of Rossini's *William Tell* Overture today without the audience laughing, and associating it with "The Lone Ranger"? One may as well play burlesque music for a performance of *Hamlet.***

* *The original score is circulated with the film at the Museum of Modern Art.*

** *Detailed commentary and analyses of this music are found in Seymour Stern's lengthy article devoted to the film in* Film Culture, *No. 36, Spring-Summer 1965, published in connection with the 50th anniversary of* The Birth of a Nation.

Two pages from the piano score of
The Birth of a Nation—music for the Klan riders
and Breil's original love theme.

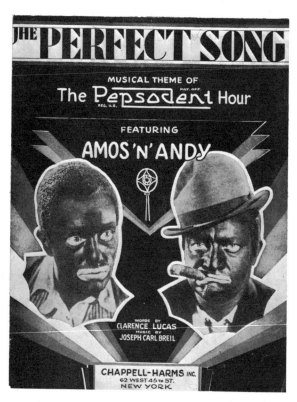

Radio's popular "The Pepsodent Hour"—featuring Amos 'n' Andy—used a musical theme five nights a week for several decades adapted from Joseph Carl Breil's original love theme for **The Birth of a Nation.**

Along with the excerpts from many composers, Breil added original themes, especially the *love strain* related to the Little Colonel and Elsie Stoneman. This theme can be played today with effect and sincerity. During the 20s and 30s it could not be included in the score with dignity because it was the nightly theme music for the *Amos and Andy* radio series. Breil published it then as "The Perfect Song." It can, however, be played today because very few people relate this music to *Amos and Andy*. Perhaps musical tastes change so rapidly and radically that the background music for such films should be changed every decade. This might not be so if the music were not so familiar. In 1915 movie audiences had no radios at home and there were no complete symphonic recordings readily available for the home phonograph. It was that year that Beethoven's Ninth Symphony was first performed west of the Mississippi.To the first audiences the score compiled for *The Birth of a Nation* seemed like a special and original work—which in many cases it was. It added scope and dramatic power to what was one of the most important films of the century. When I accompany this film today I do not use the indicated music of classical composers, but only Breil's love theme, and add the topical period tunes of the Civil War period, songs from Lincoln's day and the songs of Stephen Collins Foster. In variation and improvisation these themes magnify the film in dramatic effect and add to its epic quality.

Broken Blossoms, filmed in 1919 by D. W. Griffith, is based on Thomas Burke's story *The Chink and the Child* from a collection *Limehouse Nights*. The lead players were Lillian Gish (as Lucy, the girl), Richard Barthelmess (The Chinaman), and Donald Crisp (Battling Burrows, the prize-fighter and father of Lucy).

The film is (according to William K. Everson) as fragile as its title, a film easily shattered by insensitive audiences. A tremendously sincere film, an honestly sentimental one, it is both sensitive and poetic. Music as poetry enhances it in an ideal way, a perfect collaboration.

At the film's premier the music was arranged and composed by Louis K. Gottschalk. Score and orchestration still exist.

Because of a personal affinity to this film, I composed a new score in 1968 for the Museum of Modern Art's screenings, a score heartily approved by Lillian Gish. Portions of it follow, transcribed from tapes made of the piano version I played to complement the film at the Museum. This is illustrated in these pages to show the mood and establishment of feeling necessary for such a film. The opening music is shown. A Chinese melody in folk style begins (Invocation) at screening of the main title. This is elaborated (characteristic Chinese) dissolving into the theme representing the girl Lucy. Lucy's theme suggests a simple English folk melody in sentimental, melodic style. The girl's and the

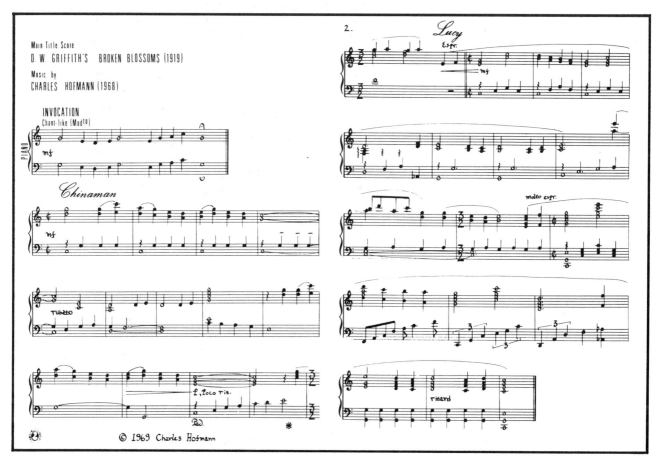

Chinaman's themes are combined as the actual film begins.

Thus is the mood established for the film. The themes recur many times in varying moods in different settings. Lucy's simple theme becomes terrifying as she is menaced and attacked by her cruel, sadistic father.

A melodramatic, but sensitive film like *Broken Blossoms* must never be over-scored, but restrained, never overdone. This is what I attempted in playing for this particular film.

A souvenir program of the premier of *Broken Blossoms* (George M. Cohan Theatre, New York City, 1919) is inscribed to me by Lillian Gish, who wrote—"who says that we tried to say, with music."

An excerpt from this music appears on the recording with this book.

Lillian Gish and Richard Barthelmess in the lead roles, and the final scene of Griffith's poetic tragedy.

Piano scores for early films in the library of the Film Department at the Museum of Modern Art have been circulated for many years when films were rented. Some of these scores are the originals as played for films when first run. Many have been compiled through the years. The current film circulating catalogue of the Museum indicates scores that are available.

Early in its years of film preservation and collection, the Museum sent the following *Suggestions for the Musical Accompaniment* with every score as an aid to the pianist.

"It is best to procure someone who has had theatrical experience to play this score. If such a person is not available, the accompanist should thoroughly familiarize himself with the music (which is usually sent out a week or so before the date of showing for this purpose)—so that on the night of the performance he may watch the screen as much as possible.

"The music is not difficult; it is made up of the familiar classics, popular songs and special 'movie music' such as was played in the silent days. However, it is difficult for one who has never done it before to play as well as watch for and catch the cues. The pianist must be alert at all times with one eye literally on the screen.

"The music is tailored to the films as closely as possible, considering that projectors are run at different speeds. In other words, when one has finished a piece and there are no repeat marks, it is usually time for the next number. At other times, the pianists will have to skip a few lines or 'stall' a bit, until the next cue, depending on the tempo of the playing and the speed of the projector. If the player hesitates and gets behind, turn over several pages in order to get in step again.

"In any case, the pianist while playing one piece should look ahead for the next cue (it is usually marked at the bottom of the page) and bear this in mind all the time in order to be ready for the change. Be careful not to change too abruptly (except in special cases). It is best to change during titles, if possible, blending the two numbers together without a long pause in between.

"It is hoped that the pianist will follow the score as closely as possible, playing the printed music which has been very carefully fitted to the period, action and moods of the films."

The music should always help the film to say what it means. Music should never impose a mood into the film that was not intended by the film-maker. The effect of a film can be completely ruined by the misuse of music. One important aspect is that the accompanying score should never make fun of the film, over-emphasizing with big effects, but underplaying, or perhaps giving the scene a boost with complementary music. The picture must be more important than the music that is accompanying it. The audience has come to see the film, not hear the score.*

* *See remarks on this subject by S. L. Rothapfel*

In more recent times film music has been given special consideration. Composers have received special awards for their contribution to films. The League of Composers in New York has presented many evenings of film music in concerts, and in 1942 sent out a questionnaire to members of the audience in its eagerness to obtain an indication of audience reaction to film music. Questions were as follows—

Do you consciously listen for film music while viewing the pictures?

Do you find film music distracting while viewing the pictures?

Do you think a good score is a necessary asset to the success of a film?

Do you think a score should be generally interpretive of the mood of the picture, or closely synchronized with the action of the film?

Do you prefer the use of familiar musical excerpts or of an original score composed especially for the picture?

Would you attend a film because of the composer's work?

Please list several motion pictures you have seen with musical scores which particularly impressed you.

Can you suggest several composers of film music whose work you would like to hear more frequently?

These questions applied to sound films with synchronized scores, many of them by eminent composers. Such questions can be applied to music for earlier films (see listings) and can be used in evaluation for preparing or hearing accompaniment to the silents.

New musical scores for early films composed or arranged during very recent years are a rarity even though there is a great need for such musical backgrounds to accompany films today.

An example comes from William Penn, graduate student (Ph.D.)* in musical composition at Michigan State University—an original piano score for the Edison film (directed by Edwin S. Porter in 1907)—*Rescued from an Eagle's Nest*. This three minute (+11½ secs.) film required seven pages of music and is reproduced following herewith. A timed cue sheet of continuity was made by Penn and corresponds to the musical sequences to accompany the film.

No one knows what music was played when Porter's *Eagle's Nest* was first shown. William Penn has recreated an older style suitable for today, recalling a type of music reminiscent of 1907. His music synchronizes with the film's fast action.

* *William Penn, being a candidate for Ph.D. degree, worked in 1968-69 on musical scores for silent films and it was agreed that his assignment for final thesis would be an original orchestral score for* The Cabinet of Dr. Caligari. *This is a cooperative project of the Department of Music at Michigan State and the College of Communication Arts (Television and Radio).*

Timing		(approximate)	Lapsed Time
:00	CUT	Log cabin; woodsman enters from cabin, followed by wife and child; kiss woodsman exits to:	:20½
:20½	CUT	Woodsmen wedging and felling a tree.	:08
:28½	CUT	Child playing in front of cabin; enter eagle; carries child away.	:31½
1:00	CUT	Close-up of eagle carrying child.	:16½
1:16½	CUT	Wife discovers the abduction; frantically points and screams.	:04
1:20½	CUT	Close-up of eagle carrying child.	:03
1:23½	CUT	Wife picks up rifle; drops rifle; in cabin to get hat; goes after husband.	:12
1:35½	CUT	Wife finds husband chopping; frantically tells him about abduction.	:10
1:45½	CUT	Men and wife lower husband down to a ledge by the eagle's nest.	:13
1:58½	CUT	Husband arrives on ledge; unties rope; finds child; sees eagle arrive; eagle swings in 3 times, last time is held, fights off eagle, eagle gets away, back again for the "big struggle"; woodsman chokes, then strikes eagle (ca. 8 times) with a tree limb; kicks eagle off ledge; embraces child.	1:08½
3:07	CUT	The END	:04½
3:11½	CUT	BLACKHAWK	:02

RESCUED FROM

AN

EAGLE'S NEST

for

PIANO SOLO

To Charles My very talented and dear friend. May we know eachother for Many years to come — WM. Penn [Kansas City '69]

by

Wm. Penn

1968

RESCUED FROM AN EAGLE'S NEST (1907)
Produced by the Edison Company
Directed by Edwin S. Porter
with
D. W. Griffith as the Woodsman

SPARSE TIMING SHEET

Timing			Lapsed Time[NB]
:00	CUT	Log cabin; woodsman enters from cabin, followed by wife and child; kiss; woodsman exits to:	:20 1/2
:20 1/2	CUT	Woodsmen wedging and felling a tree.	:08
:28 1/2	CUT	Child playing in front of cabin; enter eagle; carries child away.	:31 1/2
1:00	CUT	Close-up of eagle carrying child.	:16 1/2
1:16 1/2	CUT	Wife discovers the abduction; frantically points and screams.	:04
1:20 1/2	CUT	Close-up of eagle carrying child.	:03
1:23 1/2	CUT	Wife picks up rifle; ~~and fires~~ (~~misses~~) drops rifle; in cabin to get hat; goes after husband.	:12
1:35 1/2	CUT	Wife finds husband chopping; frantically tells him about the abduction.	:10
1:45 1/2	CUT	Men and wife lower husband down to a ledge by the eagle's nest.	:13
1:58 1/2	CUT	Husband arrives on ledge; unties rope; finds child; sees eagle arrive (eagle swings in 3 times, last time is held, fights off eagle, eagle gets away, back again for the "big struggle"); woodsman chokes, then strikes eagle (ca. 8 times) with a tree limb; kicks eagle off ledge; embraces child.	1:08 1/2
3:07	CUT	THE END	:04 1/2
3:11 1/2	CUT	BLACKHAWK	:02
3:13 1/2			

NB: Times are only approximate.

RESCUED FROM AN EAGLE'S NEST

for

PIANO SOLO

Wm. Penn

1.

2.

NB: All repeats are optional due to various editions of the film.

4.

6.

"Strangles eagle"

♩ = ca.66

Molto ritard

8va

"Hits eagle"

Allargando

Sempre forte e marcato

Molto ritard

"Eagle falls"
---Molto accel.

Simile

Sub. P

fff 8va

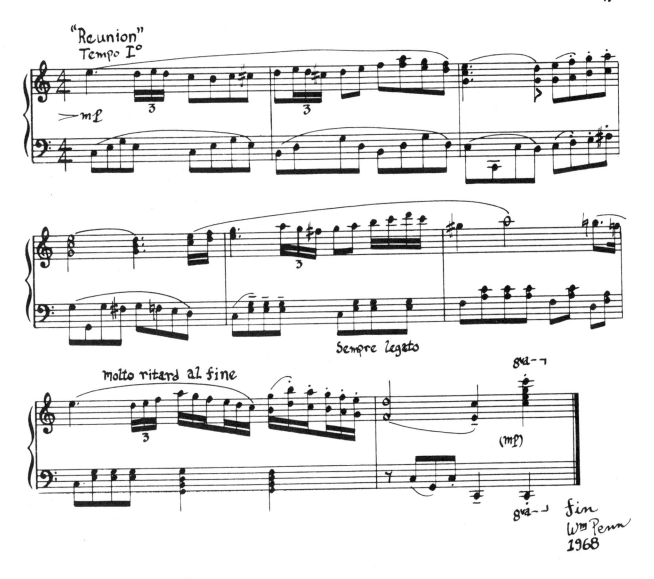

"Reunion"
Tempo I°

Sempre legato

molto ritard al fine

fin
Wᵐ Penn
1968

IMPORTANT MUSICAL SCORES FOR EARLY FILMS

L'assassinet du Duc de Guise, 1908. (Camille Saint-Saëns)
Arrah-Na-Pogue, 1911. (Walter Cleveland Simon)
The Birth of a Nation, 1915. (Joseph Carl Breil)
Intolerance, 1916. (Joseph Carl Breil)
Hearts of the World, 1918. (Carli Densmore Elinor)
Broken Blossoms, 1919. (Louis F. Gottschalk)
Foolish Wives, 1922. (Sigmund Romberg)
Orphans of the Storm, 1922. (Louis F. Gottschalk & Wm. Frederick Peters)
Puritan Passions, 1923. (Frederick Shepherd Converse)
Die Nibelungen (Siegfried & Kriemhild's Rache), 1923/24. (Gottfried Huppertz)
The Covered Wagon, 1923. (Hugo Riesenfeld)
Le Ballet Mechanique, 1924. (George Antheil)
Entr'acte, 1924. (Erik Satie)
The Thief of Bagdad, 1924. (Mortimer Wilson)
Isn't Life Wonderful?, 1924. (Cesare Sodero & Louis Silvers)
The Iron Horse, 1924. (Erno Rapee)
Greed, 1924. (Leo Kempinski)
Battleship Potemkin, 1925. (Edmund Meisel)
The Big Parade, 1925. (David Mendoza & William Axt)
The Merry Widow, 1925. (Mendoza & Axt, adapted from Lehar)
The Adventures of Prince Achmed, 1926. (Wolfgang Zeller)
Don Juan, 1926. (David Mendoza & William Axt) (Recorded Vitaphone)
Napoleon, 1926. (Arthur Honneger)
Tartuffe, 1926. (G. Becce)
Metropolis, 1926. (Gottfried Huppertz)
Ben-Hur, 1926. (David Mendoza & William Axt)
Berlin, 1927. (Edmund Meisel)
The Italian Straw Hat, 1927. (Jacques Ibert)
Sunrise, 1927. (Hugo Riesenfeld) (Recorded Fox-Movietone)
Spies, 1928. (Werner Heymann)
The Wedding March, 1928. (Louis De Francesco & L. Zamecnik)
The Patriot, 1928. (Domenico Savino & Gerard Carbonaro)
City Lights, 1931. (Charles Chaplin) (Recorded)
Tabu, 1931. (Hugo Riesenfeld) (Recorded)
Modern Times, 1926. (Charles Chaplin) (Recorded)

One of the largest collections of music for early films is found at the Museum of Modern Art. These scores, some original, some arranged in later years at the Museum, are circulated for use when films are rented from the Museum for educational screenings. These scores are sent out prior to the arrival of the film so that pianists can prepare in advance of screening. A partial listing is included here—

Great Actresses of the Past program
America (Griffith)
Animation program
Arsenal
Birth of a Nation
Black Pirate
Broken Blossoms
Cabinet of Dr. Caligari
Clever Dummy
Crazy Ray
Covered Wagon
Early Edison Shorts
Early Lumière Films
End of St. Petersburg
Enoch Arden
Entr'acte (Satie)
Fantomas
Father Sergius
A Fool There Was
Gertie the Dinosaur
Great Train Robbery
Intolerance

Iron Mask
Isn't Life Wonderful?
Last Card
Last Laugh
Mark of Zorro
Menilmontant
Metropolis
Mollycoddle
Mother
Mother and the Law
New York Hat
Orphans of the Storm
Potemkin
Assassination of the Duc de Guise &
　　Bernhardt's Queen Elizabeth
Robin Hood
Thief of Bagdad
Three Musketeers
Tol'able David
Underworld
When the Clouds Roll By
Wild and Woolly

READINGS

The following publications have references to music for early films. Books and articles usually available are devoted almost entirely to the sound film and its musical composition, recording and editing.

Beynon, George W., *Musical Presentation of Motion Pictures* (New York, G. Schirmer, 1921).

Eisler, Hans, *Composing for the Films* (New York, Oxford University Press, 1947).

Lang, Edith & George West, *Musical Accompaniment of Moving Pictures, a practical manual* . . . (Boston, Boston Music Co., 1920).

Levy, Louis, *Music for the Movies* (London, Campson Low, 1948).

London, Kurt, *Film Music* (London, Faber & Faber, 1936).

Manvell, Roger and Huntley, John, *The Technique of Film Music* (London & New York, Focal Press, 1957).

Rapee, Erno, *Encyclopedia of Music for Pictures* (New York, Belwin, 1925).

Sabaneev, Leonid, *Music and the Film* (London, Pitman, 1935).

Sinn, Clarence E., and others, eds., *Music for the Picture* (in *Moving Picture World*, November 26, 1910–March 8, 1919).

COLLECTIONS:

Suggestions for Music (Sheets for suggested music issued by the Edison Company as part of film booking service, 1910). (A cue sheet indication for the Edison film *Frankenstein* is quoted in this book.)

Zamecnik, J. S., *Sam Fox Moving Picture Music*. (Piano music for silent film accompanists. New York, Sam Fox Music Co., 1913.)

George, W. Tyacke, *Playing for Pictures*. (Guide for pianists and conductors of motion picture theatres. London, E. T. Heron & Co., 1914.)

Becce, Giuseppe, *Kinobibliothek*. (First of several volumes published in Berlin, 1919.)

Rapee, Erno, *Motion Picture Moods for Pianists and Organists*. (A rapid reference collection of selected pieces . . . adapted to fifty-two moods and situations. New York, G. Schirmer, 1924. See example in this book.)

Erdmann, H. & Becce, Giuseppe, *Allgemeines Handbuch der Film-Musik*. (Berlin, 1927.)

BIBLIOGRAPHY:

Music (Silent Era), in *The Film Index*, Vol. 1 — The Film as Art, pp. 202-207. (New York, Museum of Modern Art & H. W. Wilson Co., 1941, reprint 1966 by Arno Press.)

Photo by Lawrence Fried

THE AUTHOR

CHARLES HOFMANN is musical director of the Department of Film at the Museum of Modern Art in New York City where he can be heard at the piano with his own musical backgrounds for early films. He has lectured extensively on the subject and has been frequently heard on the CBS television series *Camera Three*.

Hofmann is also a musicologist and has lectured for several decades on music history as well as ethnic and folk music of the world. From 1945 until 1965 he lectured on these subjects at the American Museum of Natural History in New York. His specialty has been the songs and ceremonies of the American Indians, having recorded the music of fourteen tribes for the Library of Congress. His collections are available on Folkways Records and he has published three books on the subject including *American Indians Sing*.

Originator of several radio broadcast series he was heard for several years in his *Exploring Music, Singing America* and *Folk Tales Around the World*.

Hofmann has accompanied silent films at the piano since he was a teen-ager and later was heard at film festivals. He has been at the Museum of Modern Art since 1967.

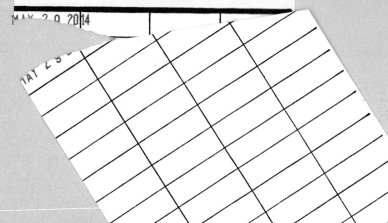
A NOTE ABOUT T

All of the recorded music w
during actual screenings of fi
The tapes were made by Mary
with the assistance of Melinda

SIDE 1:   1. THE LONEDALE C   . W. Griffith
              for Biograph, 1911, w   Excerpt.
              A young girl desperately   p on the telegraph
              at a railroad station when   is threatened by robbers.

           2. THE BIRTH OF A NATION (Directed by D. W. Griffith for
              Epoch, 1914-1915) — Opening , main title , and credits.

           3. BROKEN BLOSSOMS (Directed by D. W. Griffith for Griffith
              Productions, 1919) — Opening , main title, credits and
              opening scene.

SIDE 2:   1. THE PASSION OF JOAN OF ARC (Directed by Carl Dreyer,
              1928) — Opening scene, entrance of the judges and of Joan.

           2. PETER PAN (Directed by Herbert Brenon for Paramount, 1924,
              with Betty Bronson) — Excerpt from nursery scene, entrance
              of Tinker Bell, and Peter searching for his shadow.
              Bell, celesta and piano were used at the screening at the
              Museum in May, 1969 and the film was introduced
              by Betty Bronson.